CW00591890

Interesting Facts for Curious Folk

The most interesting book
you'll ever read.

That's a fact

MILES GOODMAN

THE OLDEST WOODEN WHEEL HAS BEEN AROUND FOR MORE THAN 5,000 YEARS

■■■■■■■■■■■■■■■■■■■■ı

Found in Slovenia in 2002, the wheel is estimated to be between 5,350 and 5,100 years old. Although old, the invention of the wheel is thought to be much earlier. It was originally invented as far back as 6,000 years ago by the ancient Mesopotamians (modern day Iraq). There is evidence to suggest that the Sumerian peoples living in the region in the 4th millennium BC, used rotating axles and solid circular wooden discs to carry heavy loads. The Slovenian wheel is an example of this type. At this time, the circular wooden discs were usually made from tree trunks. Spindled wheels came later as technology improved around 2,000 BC.

Fact 2

THE HUMAN DIGESTIVE SYSTEM COULD COVER A TENNIS COURT

You may find this fact hard to believe, but a human digestive tract is lined with small finger-like projections called microvilli, which increases the surface area for the absorption of nutrients. The human digestive tract also has a length of approximately 9 metres (30 feet). It only takes food between 24 and 72 hours to travel the entire length of the digestive system, so it has to act fast in order to grab all those essential nutrients. Interestingly, it seems that because the gut lining is so thin, it's easily damaged by an incorrect diet. Taking probiotics is said to be a good way to prevent serious damage.

Fact 3

IF YOU TRAVEL AT NEAR THE SPEED OF LIGHT, TIME WILL BE DISTORTED

This concept in physics is called 'time dilation'. The faster you travel, the slower time passes. If you travel in a vacuum (space) at 99.9% of the speed of light for 24 hours, when you return to Earth, 37 years will have passed. Imagine what everyone would look like. Interestingly, at the time of writing, the nearest Earth-like exoplanet (Proxima Centauri b) is said to be just 4 light years away. So a round trip taking you 8 years will pass around 111,000 years on Earth. Food for thought. For interest, scientists have recently discovered neutrinos that travel faster than light. If correct, it could have huge implications for physics due to breaking Einstein's theory of special relativity.

HOUSEHOLD DUST IS MADE MOSTLY OF DEAD SKIN CELLS

Your skin sheds and replaces a whopping 20,000 cells per hour. At this rate, it's no wonder your house gets so dusty. In future you may well think twice about how many guests you invite for dinner. In addition to skin cells, dust also contains a mix of bacteria, hair, clothing fibres, pollen, bits of dead insects, soil, and microscopic pieces of plastic and wood. Interestingly, the average Western household is said to accumulate and average 18 kg of dust each year. According to US census data (2017-2021) there are 124 million US households. That means generating 2.2 billion kilos of dust each year. Good job it's all biodegradable.

THE FIRST EVER ANIMATED MOVIE WAS MADE IN ARGENTINA IN 1917

Walt Disney will be turning in his grave at this fact. His 'Snow White and The Seven Dwarfs' wasn't released until 20 years later. The Argentinian film was called 'El Apóstol' and was made using 58 hand drawn sketches. The Movie was a satirical comedy based on Hipólito Yrigoyen, the Argentine president at the time. As the story goes, he dreamt about going to mount Olympus in Greece and speaking to the Gods about politics. The aim of the dream was to cleanse Buenos Aires of corruption. Sadly, the film was destroyed in 1926 by a fire.

Fact 6

SUDAN HAS MORE PYRAMIDS THAN ANY OTHER COUNTRY

When you think of pyramids, you normally think of Egypt. Of course, the most famous pyramids in the world are there on the Giza plateau, but most people don't know that Sudan is home to approximately 255 pyramids, whereas Egypt has only 118. Most were built by the 'Meriote' civilisation during a similar time period. Like in ancient Egypt, the Sudanese pyramids were built as tombs for the kings. The pyramids of Sudan are said to have smaller bases and steeper sloping sides than those further North in Egypt.

THE SMALLEST MULTICELLULAR ANIMAL IN THE WORLD IS THE TARDIGRADE

These little guys only grow up to 1.2 mm, but are as hard as nails. An experiment carried out in 2007 sent tardigrades into space to test their incredible resilience. Turns out they can survive pretty well for long periods in extreme cold and without enough oxygen. Most other life would perish in such conditions. It is estimated that the first tardigrades emerged on Earth 500 million years ago, making them the only animal to survive all 5 mass extinction events. They also comfortably outlived the dinosaurs. Would they survive a nuclear war? Most would say so.

Fact 8

ANTARCTICA IS THE LARGEST AND DRIEST DESERT IN THE WORLD

■■■■■■■■■■■■■■■■■■■■

Most people on a pub quiz would be fooled into saying the Sahara Desert for the largest and driest. They would be wrong. A desert is classified by being unable to support life by either being too hot, too cold, or having too little water. Antarctica is bitterly cold and gets less than 10 cm of rainfall per year, meaning its 3 mile deep ice sheet is mostly 'dry ice'. Most animals that live in Antarctica, live around the coastal regions and none would be able to survive the harsh conditions within. The only lifeforms you're likely to find in the central regions of Antarctica are extremophile bacteria.

Fact 9

THE TRANS-SIBERIAN RAILWAY IN RUSSIA IS THE LONGEST IN THE WORLD

The trans-Siberian railway runs from Moscow all the way to Vladivostok, passing through 87 cities and towns and 7 time zones along the way. The entire journey non-stop would take you approximately 6 days and you would travel a total of 5,775 miles. Interestingly, the railway took 25 years to build (starting in 1891) and in today's money cost approximately $25 billion. You are also able to connect with Mongolian and Chinese railways and travel all the way to Beijing (if you please). The longest bridge on the route is the Krasnoyarsk railway bridge, crossing the Yenisei river. It is just over a kilometre long. Surprisingly, it's not the longest in the world.

THERE IS ENOUGH GOLD IN THE EARTH TO COMPLETELY COAT THE PLANET

So, why is it so expensive? Well, gold in the Earth's crust is relatively fragmented and there is no one area which is gold-rich, meaning that any mining attempt would yield only small gains. Also, in the past, gold was only bought by the rich, which helped to cement its status as a sought after item. In recent years, China has been the largest producer and exporter of gold. Their contribution makes up 9% of the world's gold production. This may not sound like a lot, but it's much more than the hundreds of other countries that also mine gold.

OREOS ARE THE TOP SELLING BISCUIT IN THE WORLD

Oreos took to the shelves in 1912, but they aren't original. They were a copy of another popular biscuit called 'Hydrox Cookies'. Nevertheless, they stole the market share and now have annual sales of over 2 billion units. Sadly, according to Greenpeace, Oreos are not good for the environment. Despite being both vegetarian and vegan, the producers still buy their palm oil from Wilmar, a company that is associated with deforestation and human rights abuses in Indonesia. Popular doesn't always mean friendly.

SEAN'S BAR IS 'PROBABLY' THE OLDEST PUB IN THE WORLD

Sean's Bar in Athlone, Ireland, is the only establishment to have full ownership history dating back to 900 AD. The founders of the inn, 'Luain Mac Luighdeach' and his son acted as local guides, helping people to cross the dangerous river Shannon. This was before Athlone became an official settlement in 1129 under King Turlough O'Connor. The pub was refurbished in 1970 to remove the old 'wattle and wicker' walls and replace them with brick. They have since gained a world record for being the oldest pub in Ireland, and are currently waiting for anyone else to come forward to challenge their position as oldest in the world. Maybe another record is coming.

THE FIRST ITEM SOLD ON EBAY WAS A BROKEN LASER POINTER

One of the founders of eBay, Pierre Omidyar, set up a sale of a random broken item merely to test out the bidding system. The broken laser pen bid was won by a man who collected broken laser pens. There really is a market for anything. Pierre offered to keep the item because it was broken, but the buyer insisted. This was back in 1995. Interestingly, the highest selling items on eBay today are computer and smartphone cables. Of the 2.1 million listings, there is a success rate of 96%. Not bad considering some items don't sell at all. The most expensive thing ever sold on eBay was the Gigayacht bought by Roman Abramovich for $168 million in 2006.

Fact 14

THE DONER KEBAB ORIGINATED IN GERMANY, NOT TURKEY

∎∎∎∎∎∎∎∎∎∎∎∎∎∎∎∎∎∎∎ı

Although kebab is traditionally a Turkish invention, the doner kebab as we know it didn't gain popularity until the 1970's in Berlin, Germany. The Turkish migrant worker 'Kadir Nurman' set up a street stall in 1972, selling flatbread filled with salad and grilled meat from a rotating skewer. This stall was generally accepted as the birthplace of the doner. From there, many other Turkish migrant workers opened kebab businesses across the city. Although many other people influenced the development of the doner, Kadir is recognised by the 'Association of Turkish doner Manufacturers' as being the founder. Kadir sadly passed away in 2013 without ever obtaining a patent for his work.

Fact 15

MOST OF THE EARTH'S WATER IS NOT ACCESSIBLE TO HUMANS

■■■■■■■■■■■■■■■■■■■■■

Hard to believe, since 70% of the Earth's crust is covered in it. All ocean water is saline, meaning it's unsuitable for drinking. Only 2.5% of Earth's water is freshwater, but most of that is locked away in glaciers. This leaves only 0.007% for humans and other animals to drink. Luckily most places in the far Northern hemisphere are water-rich due to regular rainfall. Although, some more arid countries aren't so lucky and suffer regular droughts. If only there was a way to make sea water potable?! Well, this is actually possible. Australia is now the world leader in desalination practices. Following the millennium droughts, the Australian government vowed to end their water scarcity issues. They are followed closely by Israel.

Fact 16

SPAM IS NOT AN ACRONYM FOR 'SPECIALLY PREPARED AMERICAN MEAT'

∎∎∎∎∎∎∎∎∎∎∎∎∎∎∎∎∎∎∎ı

According to Hormel Foods, the company responsible for producing SPAM, the word is actually a mix of 'spice' and 'ham'. As we know the American's love mixing words. Spam was first made in July 1937, supposedly to increase the sale of pork shoulder, a cut of meat that did not sell well in butcher's shops. Hormel Foods also marketed SPAM as a health food, coining the term 'Miracle Meat'. Despite sounding ridiculous, during the second world war, SPAM did become somewhat of a miracle meat. It became a dietary staple for soldiers for many years due to its longevity inside a can. They also used the meat grease to lubricate their guns and waterproof their boots.

PEOPLE USED TO EAT ARSENIC TO IMPROVE THEIR SKIN

In the Victoria era, arsenic wafers were available to buy and were endorsed by Dr. James P. Campbell for the treatment of various skin blemishes. As you probably already know, arsenic is a poisonous metal. Ingesting too much arsenic, ironically, will cause red, swollen and itchy skin, amongst other more serious complications. Today, arsenic is only used in industry to produce pharmaceuticals, industrial chemicals and preservatives. It is also used in the making of glass. Based on those uses, it's probably not the best idea to be ingesting it.

THE TAMPAX BRAND COINED
THE TERM 'PERIOD'

■■■■■■■■■■■■■■■■■■■

In 1985, Courtney Cox of Friends was invited to do a TV
commercial for the brand. It was in that commercial
that she famously said, "using Tampax will make you
feel better about your period" (obviously meaning your
period of menstruation). This is a phrase that has stuck
with us and become commonplace. Made by Procter &
Gamble, Tampax has the global market share when it
comes to female sanitary products, with a whopping
29% monopoly. Its closest rival, Johnson & Johnson has
less than 20% share. Recently, Courtney Cox (58) has
parodied her original take on the 1985 ad, reframing it
as 'menopausal misery'. Take a look.

MORE THAN 68 MILLION PEOPLE EAT AT MCDONALD'S EACH DAY

That's the same as the entire population of the UK (2023). Given the enormous profit, it's no wonder the company opens a new restaurant every 14.5 hours and they are also the world's largest toy distributor. Interestingly, people make a living by representing the company as its mascot 'Ronald McDonald'. He will often come into restaurants for children's parties and even visit hospitals and other care facilities across the U.S. Ronald first appeared in 1963, 8 years after the company was founded in San Bernardino, California.

Fact 20

SOME SPECIES OF FUNGI ARE ABLE TO CREATE ZOMBIE ANTS

■■■■■■■■■■■■■■■■■■■■·

The parasitic fungus 'Ophiocordyceps' infects the ant's central nervous system and starts a chain of events that allow it to reproduce successfully. Once infected for some time, the fungus causes the ant to climb trees, then once at a certain height, causes it to convulse (have a fit) and fall off into the moist soil below. The ant will then die and supply nutrients for the new fungus to grow. You may worry whether this could ever happen to humans?! It is unlikely, given that this has never been seen in larger animals. It also takes millions of years for an organism to readapt to a new host. If it hasn't happened yet, then it probably won't. We have plenty of other diseases to keep us occupied.

THE SHELL OF AN ARMADILLO IS IN FACT BULLETPROOF

You may wonder how we know this. Has somebody been shooting armadillos?! Well, actually, yes. A man from Texas was hospitalised because he shot a bullet at an armadillo at close range and it ricocheted off and hit him in the jaw. The man had to have his jaw wired shut to stop the bleeding while he was airlifted to hospital. I have been unable to verify the name of the man, who probably wanted to remain anonymous since I can only imagine he would have felt mildly embarrassed following the incident.

'KLEENEX' TISSUES WERE NEVER INTENDED TO BE TISSUES

The Kleenex brand didn't come to be until the close of WWI. Kimberly-Clark, a long-established company in the toilet tissue and baby napkin market, were tasked with producing filters for soldier's gas masks. For this very purpose, they designed a thick, crepe-like, paper, which would eventually become the Kleenex tissue. As the rumour goes (although this isn't confirmed), the mask filters were not ready in time, and the war was over by the time they were developed. The company then adapted it, making a new female sanitary product called 'Kotex'. After developing a thinner tissue material from the Kotex product, Kleenex was born.

BLUE WHALES SWALLOW 500,000 CALORIES IN A SINGLE MOUTHFUL

he blue whale, the largest animal in the world, can grow up to 100 feet long. To maintain this incredible mass, they must eat an average of half a million calories with each gulp. And there's us feeling guilty after having that extra piece of cake. Interestingly, the larger an animal is, the more calories it would need to survive. Think about how many calories the dinosaurs would have needed to eat on a daily basis. Due to urbanisation and deforestation, there is no way the Earth could now support such a large animal. This is also probably one of the reasons why we don't currently have one living on land.

THE MOON IS CURRENTLY 250,000 MILES AWAY AND DRIFTING FURTHER

The moon, our guardian angel, currently sits a whopping quarter of a million miles away (which isn't far at all in space terms). If you drove a car there at 100mph, it would take you just over 104 days. Additionally, because of the collision that formed the moon, and the resulting 'sling-shot' effect, the moon still drifts 3 cm further away every year. This is approximately the same rate at which your fingernails grow. One day, the moon will be so far away that planet Earth will lose its tides, days will become longer, and the spin will lose its stability (*see fact 139 for more facts about the Earth's rotation*).

OUR NOSE AND EARS GET BIGGER AS WE AGE

I did say 'get bigger', not grow. Our nose and ears do stop growing at the same time as the rest of our bodies, but due to the pull of gravity on those particular extremities, they tend to lengthen as we age. Having said this, it would be hardly noticeable in most people. There other extremities on which the forces of gravity are more noticeable as our skin loses elasticity (bums, tums, and breasts).

THE FIRST CHRISTMAS TREES WERE INTRODUCED IN THE 19TH CENTURY

■■■■■■■■■■■■■■■■■■■'

Prince Albert, Queen Victoria's consort, was responsible for introducing the Christmas tree to the U.K. at around 1840. The U.S. followed suit shortly after. Decorating indoor trees was a popular practice in Germany (where Prince Albert was born) and was said to have begun as far back as the 16th century. Whilst talking about Prince Albert, it would be rude not to mention one of his other contributions to the world. The 'Prince Albert' piercing. Although historians cannot confirm whether this is true, one of the most firmly held rumours about him is that he had a penile piercing. True or not, this is now a household name for this type of body decoration.

THE ASTEROID THAT KILLED THE DINOSAURS COLLIDED WITH THE FORCE OF 10 BILLION ATOMIC BOMBS

It's no wonder the poor dinosaurs didn't stand a chance. Although, it wasn't the blast that killed the majority, rather the events that followed. The blast initiated deadly global firestorms, roasting many animals alive. The ejection of material (namely gypsum) from the Earth's crust also blocked out most of the sunlight, causing the Earth to enter a nuclear winter. The cold and lack of sunlight killed 70% of all plant species, leaving the remaining herbivorous dinosaurs to starve. The only remaining carnivores would have then had to rely on each other for food. Imagine the very last dinosaur battle! Little did they know it was all in vain.

THE WORLD'S LARGEST EARTHQUAKE WAS RECORDED IN CHILE IN 1960

....

This devastating earthquake was registered at a magnitude of 9.5 on the Richter scale. It is therefore known as the 'Great Chilean Earthquake'. It caused a Tsunami in the pacific ocean, which travelled at up to 200 mph and racked up quite a death toll even on faraway shores. 61 people died in Hawaii, 138 in Japan, and 32 in the Philippines (to name a few). That's not counting the people who were either killed or affected in Chile itself. Besides the death toll, the economic damage caused by the Earthquake worldwide totalled (in today's money) $4.8 billion.

AGRICULTURE INCREASED THE POPULATION WHILST DECIMATING HEALTH

Approximately 12,000 years ago, Homo sapiens began the practice of farming. Ancient farming involved the cultivation of easy-to-grow crops, such as wheat and barley, as well as keeping and breeding docile animals for meat and dairy products. There was plenty of food to go around, and supplied enough energy to keep the population alive and reproducing. Although this came at a deadly cost. Products containing wheat now make up the majority of the Western diet and are woefully poor in nutrients. Evidence now suggests that mass consumption of wheat products contributes to the onset of all modern diseases: diabetes, heart disease, cancer, and dementia.

MORE CRIMES ARE REPORTED WHEN THERE IS A FULL MOON

Does the 'Transylvania effect' actually exist? In a study running from 1978–1982, scientists looked at police data and concluded that a full moon played a role in the frequency of crime. It was also noted that the crime figures were also higher on a new moon, although still not as high as that of a full moon. It has been proposed that this is due to 'human tidal waves', where the moon's gravity pulls on the water in our bodies, altering our biological processes and ultimately our behaviour. Although the direct connection between the moon and the mind has not been proved or disproved, the connection with crime is certainly interesting to look at.

THE BEATLES HAVE SOLD MORE RECORDS THAN ANY OTHER ARTIST

A whopping 600 million records puts the Beatles on top spot. They are closely followed by Elvis Presley (500 million) and Michael Jackson (400 million). Can you guess who's next? I'll give you a clue - He's still standing. The Beatles were only active as a band for 10 years, which is quite a short time to build such a big following. The Beatles highest-selling album was Sgt Pepper's Lonely Hearts Club Band, released in 1967, selling 32 million copies. Interestingly, the only artist to sell near this many albums in the 21st Century was Adele, with her album '21', released in February 2011. She sold 31 million copies. Adele was also the highest-selling artist of 2021.

SEAWEED IS ONE OF THE MOST NUTRIENT-DENSE FOODS IN THE WORLD

Seaweed, and dark green leafy vegetables, are amongst the only foods that contain all 56 trace minerals needed for survival. It is the best source of iodine, which is essential for the correct functioning of the thyroid gland and in turn, your metabolism. It is also packed with antioxidants, which prevent damage to your DNA and could help prevent premature ageing.
Iodine is a key component in the hormone, 'thyroxine'. Thyroxine is responsible for regulating how cells metabolise most chemicals. Due to modern dietary norms, it is estimated that 30% of people are at risk from iodine deficiency worldwide.

Fact 33

THERE WAS STILL VOLCANIC ACTIVITY ON THE MOON 50 MILLION YEARS AGO

The solar system is approximately 4.5 billion years old, meaning 50 million years isn't very long in comparison. In fact, the volcanoes on the moon would have been erupting whilst the dinosaurs roamed the Earth in the late Cretaceous period 65 million years ago. There is currently no volcanic activity on the moon, although there is a lot of magma left under the lunar surface. NASA scientists have predicted that there are likely to be more minor eruptions in the future, but they are unsure when these events would happen and claim that it may not be in one human lifetime.

THE FIRST WORLD CUP WAS WON BY A ONE-ARMED PLAYER

The player went by the name of 'Hector Castro', who played as a forward for Uruguay in World Cup 1930. The final score was 4-2 to Uruguay against their neighbours and rivals, Argentina. The star was unfortunate enough to lose the arm whilst chopping up wood with an electric saw at the age of 13. Given the evidence, I'm sure he was a better footballer than he was a handyman. Good job his surname wasn't Armstrong.

NEW YORK CITY IS CURRENTLY HOME TO ALBERT EINSTEIN'S EYEBALLS

As the story goes, Einstein's autopsy was performed Illegally, and during the procedure, Thomas Harvey (the coroner) stole both his brain and his eyeballs. The eyeballs were gifted to Henry Abrams, Einstein's eye doctor, and the brain was kept for himself. The eyes remain in New York today. Anecdotally, Thomas Harvey kept the brain as he wanted to study it to find out what made Einstein such a genius. Apparently, many other scientists were also curious. Harvey dissected the brain and made it into over 1,000 microscope slides. Some are now on display at the Mutter Museum, Philadelphia. After Harvey's death in 2007, the remaining part of the brain was given to the 'University Medical Centre' in Princeton, where it now lives.

Fact 36

TENNIS BALLS USED AT WIMBLEDON NEED TO BE STORED AT 68 °F

■ ■ ■ ■ ■ ■ ■ ■ ■ ■ ■ ■ ■ ■ ■ ■ ■ ■ ■ ¡

The pressure of the air inside a tennis ball will determine how high it will bounce. To ensure consistency across matches, they are all stored at a certain temperature so bounce the same. When the balls are not too cold, the bounce will be better as there is more pressure inside the ball. This is more important when playing on softer surfaces, like grass. Interestingly, Slazenger have been supplying tennis balls to Wimbledon since 1902 and most have been white. The balls changed to yellow in 1986, and the change was said to be to increase visibility. During the tournament, used balls are sold almost daily and any proceeds go to the Wimbledon Foundation.

PREGNANCY TESTS WERE CARRIED OUT BY THE ANCIENT EGYPTIANS

. . . .

As we already know, the ancient Egyptians were no fools. They managed to build incredible monuments with only very primitive tools. Testing for pregnancy back in 1350 BC was equally as miraculous. Women would urinate on wheat and barley seeds over several days and then both sets of seeds were planted. If the wheat germinated, the baby was to be a girl, and if the barley germinated, it was to be a boy. If nothing grew, then the woman was not pregnant. This nugget of information was revealed on an ancient piece of Egyptian papyrus. Interestingly, a 1963 analysis of the method revealed that it was approximately 70% accurate.

Fact 38

NEIL ARMSTRONG'S HAIR WAS SOLD BY HIS BARBER FOR $3,000

■■■■■■■■■■■■■■■■■■■

Marx Sizemore, the Lebanese barber of Neil Armstrong, used to collect the astronaut's hair clippings after each monthly visit. The keen celebrity hair enthusiast, John Reznikoff, bought the hair from Sizemore for $3,000. After finding out about the transaction, Armstrong's attorney filed a lawsuit against Sizemore and Reznikoff. Despite proceedings, Reznikoff refused to give the hair back, but instead offered to give $3,000 to charity. After much deliberation, the Armstrong corner accepted his charitable offer. For interest, Reznikoff also has hair from other famous people: Albert Einstein, Napoleon, Abraham Lincoln, and Marylin Monroe. Each to their own.

39

THE HUMAN HEART CREATES ENOUGH PRESSURE TO SQUIRT BLOOD 30 FEET

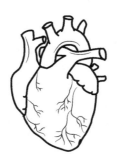

Not only does it create enormous pressure, it also pumps 5 litres of blood per minute. Interestingly, pumping blood 30 feet is not true of the resting heart. A heart at rest will only pump blood about 6 feet (sounds more reasonable). However, at the heart's maximum capacity, during exercise for example, it can do this easily. For this reason it is important that our arteries have elastic fibres in the walls so they're able to stretch each time the heart beats. This is also why calcification (or hardening) of the arteries is such a problem. The pressure the heart creates is enough to rupture an unhealthy artery which has developed an aneurysm (ballooning).

COCA COLA WAS NOT RESPONSIBLE FOR TURNING SANTA CLAUS RED

Santa Claus has been depicted many ways throughout history, although one thing we do know is that he was normally shown wearing a red jacket. However, some of his other features, we do have Coca Cola to thank for. In 1931, Coca Cola enlisted the artist 'Haddon Sundblom' to draw a version of Santa for a new TV commercial. The Santa depicted by Sundblom was a short, stocky, ageing man, with a long white beard. This image profile stuck, and is now the Santa Claus we all know and love. Maybe those asked to play Santa these days may be a little offended and want to lose a few extra pounds.

THE HEINZ SLOGAN '57 VARIETIES' IS MARKETING TOOL

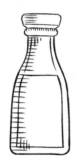

Today Heinz makes over 5,000 products that are sold globally, although '57 varieties' still appears on all of them. The simple reason will surprise you. In 1986, the founder 'H. J. Heinz' saw a very successful shoe advert on a billboard in New York city, using the slogan '21 styles' that seemed to grab the attention of passers by. It later became apparent in marketing circles that odd numbers worked better at attracting attention than even numbers did. After some thought, he decided to use his own lucky number (5) and his wife's lucky number (7) and put them together. As both were odd numbers, he knew this slogan would work to attract the attention of buyers.

MOHAMMED IS THE MOST COMMON NAME IN THE WORLD

■■■■■■■■■■■■■■■■■■■■

Obviously this is difficult to state as fact as the popularity of names change over time. However Mohammed has remained quite consistent since the dawn of the Islamic faith in approximately 610 AD. The name means 'to praise'. It's popularity is thanks to the influence of the prophet Muhammad, who was allegedly visited by the Angel Gabriel whilst on a trip to Mecca. He was informed that he was God's representative and given insights into the first teachings of the Quran. In contrast, the most common surname in the world is 'Wong'. Possibly something to do with China's vast population.

Fact 43

THE MARIANA TRENCH IS THE DEEPEST POINT OF ALL EARTH'S OCEANS

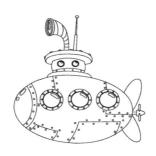

The trench is located in the Western Pacific ocean, a couple of hundred miles off the East coast of the Mariana islands. Its depth is a whopping 10,911 metres. This is enough to engulf Mount Everest, which stands at 8,848 metres. Despite the depth and enormous pressure, animals still live there. The deepest anyone had ever found a fish was at well over 6,000 metres. That was the 'Mariana Snailfish' found in 2017. The fish is capable of withstanding pressures equivalent to that of 1,600 elephants. Upon analysis, it was found that the fish's cells produced a lot of trimethylamine N-oxide (TMAO), a chemical which protects its DNA from extremely high pressures.

Fact 44

WE WERE NOT THE ONLY HUMANS ON EARTH 150,000 YEARS AGO

■■■■■■■■■■■■■■■■■■■■■

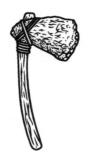

At this time, the planet was a melting pot of different human (Homo) species. Homo sapiens only became the last surviving human species as recently as 40,000 years ago, after the Neanderthals were driven to extinction. It is said that the Neanderthal extinction was due to both competition and interbreeding with Homo sapiens. It is estimated that over 100,000 years ago, there were still as many as 7 different human species walking the Earth. Palaeontologists are regularly uncovering fossil evidence linking to even more human variants, meaning our knowledge of the human lineage is being continually updated.

THE FIRST PRODUCT BARCODE SCANNED WAS WRIGLEY'S CHEWING GUM

0 0000000000 000000

The first supermarket barcode was used at Marsh's Supermarket in Troy, Ohio, on 26th June 1974. The product was a multipack of Wrigley's juicy fruit gum. Prior to this date and even beyond, the future of barcodes looked bleak. Supermarket chains were reluctant to pay for expensive scanning equipment, and manufacturers were reluctant to spend time making a complex set of codes for their inventory. Luckily, the idea caught on. A 1999 evaluation by PriceWaterhouseCoopers estimated that the universal product code (UPC) saved the grocery industry $17 billion per year (at the time of writing).

THERE ARE ONLY 10 HUMAN BODY PARTS THAT HAVE ONLY 3 LETTERS

■ ■

1. Eye
2. Ear
3. Jaw
4. Lip
5. Gum
6. Arm
7. Rib
8. Hip
9. Leg
10. Toe

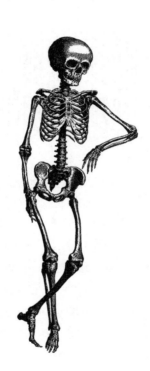

See if you can create a mnemonic to remember these.

PHYSICISTS USE THE 'KELVIN SCALE' TO MEASURE TEMPERATURE

Temperature is measured differently depending either on your profession or where you live. However, people working in physics labs across the world will always use Kelvin scale, for the following reasons. Temperature is a measure of particle vibration. Zero degrees Kelvin, or better known as 'absolute zero', is the point at which particles cease to vibrate. If particles no longer vibrate, then there is no thermal radiation coming from it. In terms of temperature, this is as cold as something can possibly be. Most of deep space is zero degrees Kelvin. For interest, this is -273 degrees Celcius, and -459 degrees Fahrenheit.

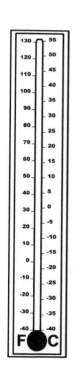

THE BRITISH EMPIRE WAS THE LARGEST IN WORLD HISTORY

■■■■■■■■■■■■■■■■■■■

By the 1920's, Great Britain controlled almost a quarter of the world's land and their populations. This equates to approximately 13.7 million square miles of territory. Over the last century, Great Britain has lost most of this territory and now only retains a few small islands, such as the Falkland islands and Bermuda. That said, King Charles is still head of state in many of the major territories. Interestingly, the second largest empire in history was the Mongol empire, although its existence was much earlier. Astonishingly, the success of an empire was usually not based on their ability to fight, but their ability to administrate. Genghis Khan's Mongolian Empire was a good example of such administrative skill.

THE EIFFEL TOWER CAN BE UP TO 6 INCHES TALLER DURING SUMMER

Heat energy from the sun causes metal particles to vibrate and require more space. If all particles need more space, then a material must get larger to accommodate. Since there is more heat in the summer months, the metal that makes up the tower can expand by a total of up to 6 inches. You may have never noticed, but this is also why joins in railway tracks have slight gaps between them, to allow for expansions in the metal due to heat. It is these gaps which give a train its characteristic banging sound whilst travelling along the rails as well as swapping tracks.

Fact 50

AUSTRALIA IS WIDER THAN THE DIAMETER OF THE MOON

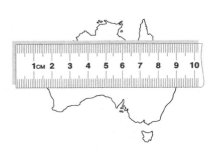

Crazy to think, since the moon looks so large in the night sky, and at 250,000 miles away (as you already know). The moon has a diameter of 3,474 km, whereas Australia has a diameter of 4,000 km at its widest point. Theoretically, it would still take more time to fly from one side of the moon to the other, than from one side of Australia to the other, due to half of the moon being more spherical than Australia. It takes 5 hours and 20 minutes to fly from Perth to Brisbane, but would take approximately 6 hours and 30 minutes to fly from one side of the moon to the other (in an aeroplane).

Fact 51

THERE IS A REAL NAME FOR TALKING RUBBISH

■ ■ ■ ■ ■ ■ ■ ■ ■ ■ ■ ■ ■ ■ ■ ■ ■ ■ ▪

An 'ultracrepidarian' is the name given to brandishing an opinion on a topic you know nothing about. Luckily, there is no ultracrepidarianism in this book. All facts have been 'fact' checked. Good for you at your next dinner party when someone tries to call bulls**t.

A BLUE WHALE'S HEARTBEAT CAN BE HEARD UP TO 2 MILES AWAY

■■■■■■■■■■■■■■■■■■■■ı

Blue whales are the largest animals on Earth and hence have the largest hearts in order to support their enormous bodies. The weight of a blue whale heart is approximately 180kg (that's about the weight of 35 tins of paint) and only beats up to 35 times per minute. Whilst diving, the whale's heart rate can go as low as 4-8 beats per minute (to save oxygen). When removed, it was found that the heart was a similar size to a golf cart. Interestingly, the initial fact is present on over 10 different websites, although none of them were able to cite where the information came from. Is this really a fact?

THE LONGEST WALK IN THE WORLD IS 14,000 MILES

o walk from Magadan, Russia to Cape Town, South \frica takes approximately 187 days non-stop (that's 1,500 hours). If you walked for a more reasonable 8 ours per day, that would extend the time to 562 days.)n route, you would pass through 16 countries and each an elevation of 117,000 metres. Some of the ransit countries may also be unsafe. Interestingly, obody has yet done this extremely long walk, probably lue to the constraints of modern life. Although, with omadic working now on the rise, this may soon hange. Would you be the first to walk this route?

IT IS ILLEGAL IN SWITZERLAND TO KEEP ONLY ONE GUINEA PIG

The Swiss government passed an animal rights law in 2008, prohibiting people from owning only one Guinea pig. The same rule applies to parrots. Because both species are social animals, it is considered abusive if they aren't allowed to interact with other Guinea pigs and parrots. Since the law was passed, there is an agency which now specialises in finding friends for lonely Guinea pigs, if a family were to lose one. Interestingly, this isn't the only animal-friendly law that Switzerland has passed. It is now a legal requirement for prospective dog owners to take a course in how to look after their dog. Swiss fishermen also must take a course on humane fishing practices.

WE 'RAISE A TOAST' THANKS TO THE ANCIENT ROMANS

For good health, the ancient Romans used to drop a piece of burnt toast into their wine. The alleged reason for this was that the toast would help temper some of the bad wine they had to drink. The carbon would also help to reduce the acidity of the wine, making it easier to drink. This was known as a 'tostus'. Interestingly, there are many other reasons why we 'cheers', some of which are folklore. In mediaeval Europe, the easiest way to kill someone (and get away with it) was to poison their drink. People used to 'clink' tankards so hard that part of the drink would spill over into the other person's vessel. If someone wouldn't 'cheers', they were seen as an enemy and possibly a murderer.

THE FIRST POWERED AIRCRAFT TOOK TO THE SKY ON 17TH DECEMBER 1903

■■■■■■■■■■■■■■■■■■■ı

Wilbur and Orville Wright were American inventors and engineers. They began their career developing and repairing bicycles after opening their first shop in 1892. Bicycles brought the Wright brothers substantial wealth, which allowed them to pursue their interest in flight. Inspired by the first flight of an unmanned motorised aircraft by the Smithsonian Institution in 1892, the Wrights began to experiment with various similar designs. They first engineered and built a series of gliders in order to gain insight into wing controls and lift. Once they had the design ready, a purpose built engine was made in their bike shop. After many delays, the Wright's eventually flew into the record books on 17th December 1903.

Fact 57

ART USED TO BE A COMPETITIVE SPORT IN THE OLYMPICS

This only lasted for 36 years before it was abolished from the Olympics. Events used to include sculpting, painting, architecture and music. At the 1912 Olympics in Stockholm, Walter Winans was awarded a gold medal for a 12-inch sculpture of a gold horse pulling a chariot. Jack Yeats, an Irish painter was also awarded a silver medal in the Paris 1924 Olympics for his famous painting 'The Liffey Swim'. It was around this time that artists began to paint and sculpt sporting scenes in an attempt to keep art relevant. As sport was slowly taking over, art and literature sadly became a 'laughable' side-show. In 1952, art and literature was removed from the Olympics all together. Would you like to see it reinstated?

Fact 58

TWO PEOPLE MATCHED ON TINDER IN ANTARCTICA IN 2013

In 2013, an American male scientist (who will not be named) was working out at the McMurdo research station on Ross Island, Antarctica. Probably out of boredom, he opened up Tinder to see if anyone else there was looking for love. He was surprised to find a match with one lady, who was also stationed in Antarctica, some 45 minutes away by helicopter. The lady (who also is not named) was camping in Antarctica's Dry Valleys conducting research at the time of the match. The couple did chat and meet up briefly, but she had to leave shortly after. The couple are hopeful that they will get a chance to meet again and spend more time getting to know each other. What a story for the grandchildren!

THE MOST EXPENSIVE BOTTLE OF WINE SOLD PRIVATELY FOR $1 MILLION

You might ask, "What does it take to give a wine that kind of price tag?" Well, this one was aged in space. The 2000 Chateau Petrus spent over a year orbiting the Earth on the International Space Station. Interestingly, that price was just for the bottle of wine that was sold in May 2021. The offering also included a hand-crafted trunk that was designed by 'Maison D'artist Ateliers' and street artist 'Cyril Kongo'. The final price for the set was not disclosed. The only bottle of alcohol which has fetched more at auction was a bottle of champagne in 2022, which went for $2.5 million. As with the former, there was much more to that bottle than just the liquid.

VENUS IS THE ONLY PLANET IN THE SOLAR SYSTEM TO SPIN CLOCKWISE

∎∎∎∎∎∎∎∎∎∎∎∎∎∎∎∎∎∎ı

Although it is not clear exactly why this is the case, the generally accepted reason is that it may have originally spun anticlockwise but was hit by another celestial body, which changed its rotation. This of course has no impact on habitability as Venus is one of the most hostile environments we know of. The surface temperature is over 400°C in both the day and night. As this is too hot to maintain liquid water, most exists as vapour in Venus's thick carbon dioxide atmosphere. Due to extensive volcanic activity, the atmosphere is full of sulphur dioxide, which dissolves in the water vapour, making thick sulphuric acid clouds. In addition, the air pressure is 100x greater than Earth's. Not the most welcoming of places.

Fact 61

GOOGLE IMAGES WAS CREATED BECAUSE OF JENNIFER LOPEZ

At the year 2000 Grammy's, Jennifer wore an iconic green 'Versace' dress that so many people were searching on google, they decided to make an image search page to easily display the same images from various sources. Developers at Google noted in 2000 that there were more searches for Lopez's dress than anything else in Google history. They tasked a new developer and production manager to work on the project, successfully releasing Google images on 12th July 2001. By the end of that year, 250 million images had been indexed, rising to 1 billion images by 2005. The reverse image functionality was the last to be added in 2011.

THERE IS A FRUIT THAT TASTES LIKE CHOCOLATE PUDDING

■ ■ ■ ■ ■ ■ ■ ■ ■ ■ ■ ■ ■ ■ ■ ■ ■ ■ ■ ı

Black Sapote is a fruit native to Mexico, Central America, and Colombia. When ripe, it is said to taste like a mix of caramel and cocoa. It is about the size of a tomato and has soft flesh similar to that of a papaya. People have commented that the flavour is similar to that of a date or prune. Although, this is only the case when the fruit is ripe (when deep green coloured). If the fruit is not ripe it can often taste bitter and caustic. Unripe fruits have also been used in the Philippines to poison fish, although there is little danger to humans from eating unripe sapote. As with many fruits, sapote is also highly nutritious, containing both vitamin C and calcium.

THE VOICE ACTORS OF MICKEY AND MINNIE MOUSE WERE MARRIED

The late Wayne Allwine was the third voice of Mickey Mouse, after Jimmy MacDonald and Walt Disney himself. He played the character from 1977 until his death in 2009. During his career as Micky he met Russi Taylor, the voice of Minnie Mouse. Russi began in the role in 1986. Needless to say, the fictional couple hit it off in real life and ended up marrying in 1991. Russi continued to voice Minnie Mouse for 10 years after Allwine's passing. The couple had no children, but Wayne did have four of his own from a previous marriage. The couple received the status as 'Disney Legends' in 2008, the company's Hall of Fame program for long-standing service.

HOMEWORK ORIGINATED IN GERMANY AFTER UNIFICATION

■ ■ ■ ■ ■ ■ ■ ■ ■ ■ ■ ■ ■ ■ ■ ■ ■ ■ ▪

Many bloggers speak of the mythical Italian, 'Roberto Nevilis' who allegedly gave his students work to do at home because of poor class performance in 1905. Although, this cannot be proved by literature. The real homework story began in the late 19th century with 'Horace Mann', a politician who had a fascination with post-unification education in Germany. Students attending the Volksschule (people's school) were regularly given assignments to do in their own time. Despite its sinister nature (that of the government asserting dominance over people at a volatile time), the idea swiftly caught on. Homework rapidly spread across Europe and eventually reached the US.

QUEEN ELIZABETH II WAS A VEHICLE MECHANIC DURING WORLD WAR 2

At the age of 19, the late Queen Elizabeth (then Princess of Wales) joined the Auxiliary Territorial Service (ATS). There she was trained in truck repair - including engines and tyres. Her younger sister Margaret was too young to serve in the military but was a girl guide at the time. Their father, George VI, held his position as Marshal of the RAF and almost always appeared in uniform. His wife, the Queen Mother, refused to leave Buckingham Palace, even though it was bombed repeatedly. She insisted that they must stay to show solidarity to the people of the UK. Elizabeth became queen of England in 1952, following the death of her father George VI to smoking-related illness.

MOST PROBIOTIC YOGHURTS DON'T HAVE ANY HEALTH BENEFITS

∎∎∎∎∎∎∎∎∎∎∎∎∎∎∎∎∎∎∎ı

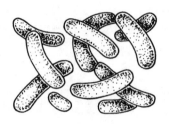

Clever marketing ensures that we all know how important it is to have good bacteria in our gut. Interestingly, this has become even more important due to recent scientific studies, indicating that good bacteria can regulate both mood and metabolism and also prevent early onset of age related diseases. Interestingly, buying probiotic yoghurts has been shown to be a waste of time, as most of the live Lactobacillus bacteria are killed by your stomach acid and never make it to the intestines, where they are needed. If you're interested in probiotics to improve gut health, it is better to purchase spore forming bacteria like 'Bacillus coagulans'. Bacterial spores are not affected by stomach acid.

THE CHUPA CHUPS LOGO WAS DESIGNED BY SALVADOR DALI

■■■■■■■■■■■■■■■■■■■■ı

The artist better known for his surrealist melting objects actually designed the logo for the Spanish lollipop company in 1969. Since then, Chupa Chups have not changed this iconic logo, despite the fact that it only took Dali one hour to design and he was paid millions of dollars for his trouble. Although, he did contribute to the product's marketing by suggesting that the logo be on the top of the lollipop so it was always visible to the buyer. Interestingly, Chupa Chups now has over 2,000 employees and 99% of their sales are made outside of Spain. The company has a yearly revenue of $441 million.

A 'JIFFY' IS A REAL UNIT OF TIME

We've all used the phrase, "I'll be back in a jiffy". Although, I bet nobody has actually given a second thought to how long that may be (if nothing more than a short time). This is correct, as a jiffy is now universally accepted as being 1 hundredth of a second. Sounds small, but is ten times bigger than a millisecond. Historically, the jiffy has been used differently depending on the field of study. Initially it was the time taken for light to travel one centimetre. It was then used in electronics to measure A.C. current power cycles. Then in computing to measure the time between two ticks of a system timer interrupt. It certainly took more than a jiffy to find all of this information.

THERE IS A 'GLAM CLAUSE' IN KIM KARDASHIAN'S WILL

The TV celebrity is so vain it seems, that she has written into her will that if she is ever unconscious, unable to get dressed, unable to do her makeup, hair, and nails by herself, then somebody must do it for her before she is seen by the public. I wonder who is 'on hand' in case she ever becomes incapacitated?! For interest Kim Kardashian owns a number her own beauty brands, so therefore makes sense that she must always be #flawless. She is currently in the process of rebranding so all her lines come under a single brand. She insists that the removal of the 'KKW' makeup brand is nothing to do with her divorce from Kanye West, which finalised in 2022.

THE LETTER 'J' WAS THE LAST TO BE ADDED TO THE ENGLISH ALPHABET

The letter 'J' wasn't added to the English alphabet until 1524. Before this time, people would use an elongated letter 'i' to indicate the sound of a 'J'.

Interestingly, the most commonly used vowel in the English alphabet is 'E', and most commonly used consonant is 'R'. Also, more English words begin with the letter 'S' than any other letter.

HUMANS ARE THE ONLY ANIMALS TO COOPERATE 'FLEXIBLY' ON MASS

here is one ability above all that allows humans to dominate the planet. The ability to cooperate flexibly in large numbers. Other animals are also able to cooperate flexibly, but can only do so within small family groups (animals they know well). Alternatively, a beehive is a great example of mass cooperation, but it's very inflexible. There is no other animal that has yet been seen to achieve both. It is proposed that humans gained this ability through the collective belief in fictional stories – religious teachings, gods, laws, money, all work to enable a mass cooperation network. These are all things that do not exist in another animal's strictly objective world.

Fact 72

SLEEP IS MORE IMPORTANT TO THE BODY THAN FOOD

....

Why would nature have us do something that disables all of our other survival functions?! Must be important, right?! It actually has more benefits than you would believe. In short, without proper sleep you would be dead within approximately 8 weeks, suffering a multitude of ails in the interim. There are two types of sleep: NREM sleep and REM sleep. NREM sleep is responsible for keeping your organs and metabolism in a healthy state. REM sleep is responsible for your emotional stability. Interestingly, there is a condition called 'fatal familial insomnia' where a person completely loses the ability to sleep and will die within weeks.

Fact 73

SPICE GIRLS SOLD MORE RECORDS THAN ANY OTHER GIRL BAND

The girls had a career spanning over 10 years and have sold over 100 million albums to date. This makes them the most successful British pop group since The Beatles. Not only did the Spice girls sell a lot of records, they were also role models for women and stood for female empowerment and solidarity. They also paved the way for other all-female pop groups, changing the trajectory of the music industry. Interestingly, despite the Spice girls' sales success, the girl group 'Bananarama' have spent more time in the top 40 charts than any other girl band, including Spice Girls. After 35 years, Bananarama have been hailed as the biggest girl band since The Supremes.

Fact 74

THE WORLD'S SHORTEST WAR LASTED 45 MINUTES

The Anglo-Zanzibar war fought in 1896 lasted between 38 and 45 minutes, making it the shortest war in recorded history. The war was fought between the United Kingdom and the 'unofficial' Zanzibar sultan, Khalid bin Barghash. Barghash assumed power after the sudden death of the British-endorsed sultan, Hamad bin Thuwaini. It is still unknown whether Hamad was poisoned by Khalid due to his pro-British sentiments, although this is assumed to be the case. Nevertheless, within 45 minutes of the announcement, the palace was surrounded by British forces, causing Barghash to flee to safety. The palace was then destroyed and the Barghash flag was taken down.

ON A PLANE YOU ARE IN FACT BREATHING CLEAN AIR

■■■■■■■■■■■■■■■■■

Most people worry about breathing recycled air whilst on a plane, but this isn't necessarily true. At least 60% of plane cabin air is brought in from outside and pressurised before reaching the cabin. Only 40% of the air needs to be put through a HEPA (high-efficiency particulate air) system to remove any dangerous microbes. With 60% being fresh air, the air in the cabin is completely replaced every three minutes. Although it is true that having a lot of people in such a confined space is more likely to spread infection, this is only a result of your proximity to the infected person, not the air on the plane.

Fact 76

EATING FAT DOESN'T MAKE
YOU FAT

■■■■■■■■■■■■■■■■■■■■

Since the 1950's when president Dwight Eisenhower suffered a heart attack, the U.S. department of health has waged war on dietary fats. Supposed 'healthy' foods have replaced much of the fat with more sugars (in order to keep the taste). Since this time, the rate of heart disease has not decreased, and the rate of obesity has almost doubled. So what is to blame? Possibly sugar? Insulin is a hormone responsible for keeping our blood sugar level correct. It also is responsible for up-regulating the storage of fat. Interestingly, eating fat does NOT cause an increase in insulin (or fat storage), whereas eating sugars and complex carbohydrates certainly does. Keep eating those good fats.

Fact 77

THE FIRST SPEEDING TICKET WAS ISSUED IN THE UK IN 1896

Whilst waging war on rogue sultans in Zanzibar, UK police were also issuing the first speeding tickets to citizens back home. 'Walter Arnold' was the first person to ever receive a speeding fine. The daft part of this story is that Walter was pelting a measly 7mph through Paddock Wood in Kent. The speed limit at the time was only 2mph and Arnold was fined just £7 after being chased down by a policeman on a bicycle. Walter Arnold was one of the first 'horseless carriage' dealers in the UK and worked for the German manufacturer, Benz motors, as well as starting his own carriage company. As you would imagine, Arnold was not short of money and could easily pay the fine.

PEAR CIDER DOES NOT EXIST

∎∎∎∎∎∎∎∎∎∎∎∎∎∎∎∎∎∎∎∎

Cider, by definition, is the fermentation of apples and nothing else. So, to say you are having a pear cider is always incorrect. Although, what you did have when you thought you had pear cider was actually a drink called 'perry', made from fermented pears. So, why was it sold to you as pear cider?! Well, perry drinks went out of fashion. Then as ciders increased in popularity, someone cleverly rebranded the fermentation of other fruit drinks as 'ciders'. Interestingly, the world's best selling pear cider today is the Swedish, Kopparberg. In contrast, Strongbow is still the overall top selling cider brand worldwide.

SNAILS SLEEP FOR LONGER THAN ANY OTHER ANIMAL

Unlike other animals that hibernate in winter, snails sometimes go into what's called 'summer sleep'. This is because snails need to retain moisture. If the weather is hot and dry they will risk losing water from the skin. So this doesn't happen, they will cover themselves in a layer of mucus and go to sleep. Such moisture and energy conserving sleep can last for up to three years. Although, when the weather is cooler, snails do revert back to a more regular sleep pattern, like that seen in other animals. Interestingly, snails rely on moisture to form the characteristic 'snail trails'. Without them they wouldn't be able to move.

PINEAPPLE IS A NATURAL MEAT TENDERISER

If you want nice tender meat in your stew, best to leave it soaking in some pineapple for a while. Pineapple contains the enzyme 'bromelain', which breaks apart protein chains, making meat softer to the touch. If you are unlucky enough to be exposed to bromelain for prolonged periods, you may develop sores on the skin as it is breaking down the protein fibres in your hands. Best to be aware of this fact if you work in a tinned fruit factory. Interestingly, when absorbed by the digestive tract, bromelain has some surprising health benefits, including anticoagulant and anti-inflammatory properties. It is also said to protect against cardiovascular disease.

M&M'S WERE NAMED AFTER THE MEN THAT INVENTED THEM

Inspired by their rival, Smarties, M&M's were first made and sold in 1941. They were produced by Bruce Murray and Forrest Mars. Forrest was the son of Frank C. Mars (of the now famous 'Mars incorporated' brand). M&M's were initially sold only to the U.S. armed forces, due to being robust sweets that were largely resistant to heat. Following increasing popularity within the forces, they began to be sold to the general public. By 1949, Mars had bought Murray out of the company and M&M's were taken back under the Mars corporation umbrella, whilst keeping their original name.

Fact 82

FAIRGROUND CANDY FLOSS WAS INVENTED BY A DENTIST

■ ■ ■ ■ ■ ■ ■ ■ ■ ■ ■ ■ ■ ■ ■ ■ ■ ■ ■ ı

Interesting stuff. Maybe the dentist, William Morrison, was a little short of customers at his practice. It is still not known exactly what his motivations were for the creation, nevertheless, he did create something magical that is now enjoyed at fairgrounds across the world. He and his business partner, John Wharton (a candy-maker), developed the candy floss machine in 1897. The machine consists of a spinning bowl filled with tiny holes. Sugar is then heated (to caramelise) and fed through the holes, coming out as tiny strands similar to cotton. It is then wound many times around a wooden stick.

THE WORD 'SET' HAS MORE MEANINGS THAN ANY OTHER WORD

Since the 1989 edition of the Oxford English dictionary, the word 'set' has had 430 definitions. The dictionary entry itself is 30,000 words long and holds the record for the longest ever. A great way to 'set' a world record. It really 'sets' the standard for English words. We should 'set' up a site to see how many sentences we can make with the word 'set'. You get the idea... For interest, set is followed by 'go', with 368 definitions.

Fact 84

SUPERMAN DIDN'T ALWAYS FLY

■■■■■■■■■■■■■■■■■■

In the original books, Superman was able to jump from building to building, but didn't have the ability to fly. Most people think the new superpower was given to him by 'Fleischer Studios' when they made the first Superman animations back in the 1940's. Although, this is not factually correct according to the Superman website. Superman did actually fly in the comic books prior to the first animations of the character. Although as the fact suggests, this was still not the intention. Superman's flight was an error by the comic artist 'Leo Nowak' in 1939. He was said to be a little too 'enthusiastic' about the character and drew him flying, not jumping.

BANGING YOUR HEAD AGAINST A WALL BURNS 150 CALORIES PER HOUR

Good to know if you're having one of those days. At least your anguish is keeping you fit. This is the same as running for approximately 10 minutes, or walking briskly for 30 minutes. Of course, banging your head against a wall isn't recommended due to possible brain damage. Running or walking is definitely safer, less painful, and more effective. Alternatively, you could also just stand for a few hours and see the same benefits.

THE IRRATIONAL FEAR OF HAPPINESS IS CALLED 'CHEROPHOBIA'

We need to be careful about spreading cheer when these people are around. Any situation that would be deemed fun by most, would cause a cherophobia sufferer a fair amount of anxiety. The term actually comes from ancient Greece – the word 'chero' means to rejoice. People suffering from cherophobia will often avoid situations that many would see as fun. Interestingly, although this condition definitely exists, it is understudied. Additionally, the condition isn't yet named in the Diagnostic and Statistical Manual of Mental Disorders (DSM-5). Luckily it doesn't affect too many people.

Fact 87

SMALLPOX WAS COMPLETELY ERADICATED BY 1976

Through successful vaccination programmes around the world, smallpox is no longer with us. The last case was seen on 25th October 1975. Worryingly, there is now much more hesitation when it comes to getting vaccinated. This is primarily due to misinformation circulating on social media. Many new studies have demonstrated a strong link between increased disease incidence and circulating misinformation. It was also noted that those who refused vaccination were also more likely to post misinformation. It would do us all well to remember that the deadly smallpox would certainly still be with us if it wasn't for vaccination.

THE MOST RELIABLE CAR BRAND IN THE WORLD IS TOYOTA

■ ■

Arguably not the most 'cool' of cars, but the Japanese giant, Toyota, is certainly up there when it comes to reliability. If you look at any online car reliability survey, or warranty statistics, you will usually find a Toyota car ranking in the top 5. A useful fact if you want to save some money in car maintenance. Other reliable brands include the Korean, Kia and Hyundai, and the Romanian Dacia, which also score highly. Interestingly, the Lexus (Toyota's luxury brand) LC 400 has been named one of the most reliable cars of all time. At the other end of the spectrum, the least reliable cars are said to be Jeep and Land Rover.

A COLOSSAL SQUID HAS THE LARGEST EYES IN THE WORLD

∎∎∎∎∎∎∎∎∎∎∎∎∎∎∎∎∎∎∎ı

It's hard to see in the sea, especially the deeper you go. The giant squid's eyes are perfectly adapted for this dark environment. They are about the same size as a football (approximately 10 inches in diameter). The squid also has photophores (like biological headlights) at the back of its eyes, allowing it to see better in the dark. It is thought that this is a common feature of animals that lurk at such depths. The giant squid would normally be found at 1000m or even deeper in the Southern Ocean. Much like the Mariana Snail Fish, the Colossal Squid has a lot of trimethylamine N-oxide (TMO) in its body to counteract the water pressure.

THE FIRST SLICED BREAD WAS SOLD IN 1928

The bread slicing machine was invented by the inventor, Otto Rohwedder, in 1927. Not only did it slice the bread, it also bagged it. Genius! Otto's friend, Frank Bench, was a baker at the 'Chillicothe Missouri Bakery' who agreed to try it out at his store. Obviously, they all agreed it was the best thing since.......?? A few years later another Missouri baker, Gustav Papendick, improved the packaging part of Rohwedder's design, keeping the bread fresh for longer. The first corporation to sell sliced bread was the 'Continental Baking Company' when they released their novel 'Wonder Bread' in 1930. The rest is history.

Fact 91

SINGAPORE AIRLINES RUNS THE WORLD'S LONGEST DIRECT FLIGHT

With aircraft now being more efficient (and reliable) than ever, it is possible to run routes which were not possible just a few years ago. 'Singapore Airlines' - New York to Singapore is the longest direct flight route in the World, lasting 18 hours and 50 minutes. For this route the company uses the new Airbus A350-900, with Rolls Royce Trent XWB-84 engines, the most fuel-efficient aircraft engines on the market. Even though the A450-900 is as efficient as they get, a flight this long will still burn 125,000 litres (27,500 gallons) of aviation fuel. Sounds a lot but between 350 passengers, that's 122 mpg (per person), similar to a highly efficient car.

THE SANDWICH WAS INVENTED IN 1762

I bet you can't guess how the sandwich was created?! John Montagu, the 4th Earl of Sandwich, was an avid gambler. One day, he was so engrossed in a game that he refused to leave the gambling table to eat. Instead he asked his butler for a serving of roast beef between two slices of bread, so he could eat with his hands whilst continuing to play. The tradition quickly caught on and the sandwich was born. There is now a restaurant chain named 'The Earl of Sandwich' in his honour. The company was founded in Orlando, Florida, by the 11th Earl of Sandwich (also John Montagu) and his son Orlando Montagu.

Fact 93

CATS HAVE 32 MUSCLES IN EACH EAR

■ ■ ■ ■ ■ ■ ■ ■ ■ ■ ■ ■ ■ ■ ■ ■ ■ ■ ı

Despite this, our feline friends are still very good at ignoring us. A cat's hearing is one of the best in the animal kingdom. Cats, particularly smaller breeds, are both predators and prey. It is therefore particularly important that they can hear well to listen out for predators. A cat's hearing frequency range is larger than that of both humans and dogs, ranging from 45 Hz to 64 kHz. For comparison, a human's hearing range is between 20 Hz and 20 kHz. Cats can also move each ear independently, which humans and most other animals can't. Additionally, many people think that cats can hear ultrasound machines. This is false.

THE LONGEST VERIFIABLE HUMAN LIFETIME WAS 122 YEARS

■ ■ ■ ■ ■ ■ ■ ■ ■ ■ ■ ■ ■ ■ ■ ■ ■ ■ ı

'Jeanne Louise Calment' from France holds the record for the longest verified lifetime. Jeanne was born in 1875 and died in 1997. When interviewed, Jeanne claimed that her secret to longevity was a diet of chocolate, olive oil, and port wine. No surprise, considering that cocoa and red wine both contain many anti-ageing polyphenols. Olive oil also promotes digestive and cardiovascular health. In contrast, she did also smoke, but not a lot.

Fact 95

GOOGLE USED TO BE CALLED BACKRUB

he Backrub search engine began in 1996 as a research project. The engine would use the quantity and quality of internet backlinks to rank the importance of certain ey terms. It was engineered and built by Larry Page nd Sergey Brin, two students of Stanford University, in he UK. After a short time, Backrub was changed to the ame 'Google', a mathematical wordplay on 'Googol' neaning 10 to the power 100, or an unfathomable umber. After just a few years of successful trialling of he software, the search engine caught the eye of nany Silicon Valley investors, including Jeff Bezos. I'm unning out of space, but if you want to know more, you ould Google it.

BARBIE'S FULL NAME IS BARBARA MILLICENT ROBERTS

■■■■■■■■■■■■■■■■■

The Barbie doll was named after the daughter of her creator, Ruth Handler, although the middle and surname are not the same. Interestingly, she also had a son called Kenneth Handler, who would become the 'Ken' doll. Most people who play with Barbie and Ken think they're in love, but in reality, they were brother and sister. Barbie was first made on 9th March 1959 and I guess you could call that her birthday. She is 64 years old (in 2023). Interestingly, if you wanted to pick up an original Barbie doll from 1959, you could be paying anywhere between $8,000 and $27,000.

Fact 97

THE MOSQUITO IS THE DEADLIEST ANIMAL IN THE WORLD

■ ı

Forget about sharks and venomous snakes; the mosquito kills more people each year than any other animal. Not directly of course, as the mosquito itself is harmless. However, they can carry a whole host of deadly pathogens. Malaria, caused by the *plasmodium* parasite, kills more people each year than any other disease (619,000 in 2021). The countries with the highest prevalence of malaria are in Central and Western Africa, with 80% of deaths being children under 5. There are also many other potentially dangerous diseases carried by mosquitoes, such as African sleeping sickness, which is fatal in most cases. Dengue fever and West Nile Virus can also cause serious illness.

Fact 98

IT IS DIFFICULT TO BUY DEODORANT IN THE REPUBLIC OF KOREA

■■■■■■■■■■■■■■■■■■■■

Most people born in far Eastern countries are missing a specific gene that codes for armpit odour. The gene is called ABCC11. Upon investigation, the South Koreans were found to have the lowest prevalence of this gene amongst all East Asian populations – the gene was expressed in only 0.006% of people. Interestingly, this same gene also controls whether a person has hard or soft earwax. People either have soft earwax and body odour (ABCC11+), or hard earwax and no body odour (ABCC11–). Getting an ancestry DNA test will usually tell you whether you're positive or negative. Unless you already know because you've smelt your body odour.

Fact 99

MISS PIGGY AND YODA WERE VOICED BY THE SAME PERSON

The voice actor, Frank Oz, is responsible for both of the characters' distinctive voices. Frank was a well-known puppeteer and began working on the Muppet Show at the age of 19, where he performed the voice of Miss Piggy and others. In 1980, he was approached by George Lucas and asked to be puppeteer and voice for the Yoda character in the film 'Empire Strikes Back'. Whilst playing the character, it was Frank who gave Yoda many of his character traits, such as speaking in riddles. Frank continued to perform the voice of Yoda in all of the main Star Wars films, including the prequels from 1999-2005. "Performed well he did".

ARNOLD SCHWARZENEGGER WAS THE YOUNGEST EVER MR UNIVERSE

Arnold Schwarzenegger won Mr Universe for the first time at the age of 20. He then went on to win the competition a further three times, before quitting bodybuilding at age 33. Interestingly, whilst all this was happening, Arnold also had a successful brick-laying business, based in California. Arnold had always dreamt of leaving Austria, due to terrible abuse he suffered at the hands of his father, a police chief who supported the Nazi's during WWII. Following his success as a bodybuilder, Arnold also had an illustrious film career and is now worth an estimated $450 million. At least a terrible upbringing did one good thing in making Arnold such a determined character.

THE MATRIX CODE IS ACTUALLY MADE FROM JAPANESE SUSHI RECIPES

Simon Whiteley, the creator of the infamous green matrix code, actually stole the symbols from his Japanese wife's sushi cookbook. Very creative some might say. When we saw the code pouring across the screen in the movie, we were all wondering what it meant for Neo and Trinity in the computer generated world. Now it seems it was probably just somebody making a vegetable maki roll. Simon began working on the digital rain scene from the movie after the directors (Lilly and Lana Wachowski) didn't like the original version made by the design team. They felt the original design wasn't 'Japanese or manga enough', so needed another perspective.

THE MERGING OF TWO WORDS IS KNOWN AS A 'PORTMANTEAU'

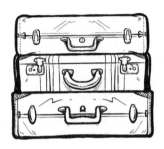

We should go and 'chillax' somewhere and have some 'brunch' before heading to the 'motel'. You get the idea. This merging of words, not only is incredibly annoying, it also has a name that nobody knows or uses. Interestingly, the name 'portmanteau' also refers to a large double-sided suitcase.

POINTING THE CAR FOB AT YOUR HEAD INCREASES ITS RANGE

■ ▪

This sounds like a fallacy, but this has been tried many times and been proven true. It was famously done on Top Gear by Jeremy Clarkson. The reason behind it is quite complex but in simple terms, the water inside your body acts as an amplifier for the signal. This also works if you hold the fob next to a container of water. Because the water in your body is inside a cavity, when you administer electromagnetic waves (radio in this case) to it, a 'dielectric resonator' is created, which increases the amplitude of the waves making them travel further.

VEGETABLES AND FRUITS DON'T EXIST IN BIOLOGY

According to botanical experts, using the terms 'vegetable' or 'fruit' are misnomers. When classifying organisms, we use the Linnean naming system. For example, humans are in the family, 'animalia' along with all other animals. Although, there is no family in the plant kingdom for vegetables or fruit. They are all members of different plant families. Vegetables and fruits are really only named as such for culinary purposes, usually by their basic defining features. Fruits usually come from the flower of the plant and contain seeds, whereas vegetables are from any other part of the plant and are generally seedless.

THE WORD 'ASTRONAUT' CAN BE TRANSLATED TO 'STAR SAILOR'

Star sailor sounds much cooler than 'astronaut' if you ask me. The word is actually a compound word originating from ancient Greek. The word 'astro' means star, and 'naut' means sailor. Yuri Gagarin of Russia was the world's very first Star Sailor, who went into space on 12th April 1961. This achievement was part of what we now call the space race between the US and USSR during the cold war. The US eventually prevailed in 1969 by landing the first man on the moon. Interestingly, following the moon landing, interest in space exploration dwindled and we are only just recovering our interest in sending people back to the moon.

Fact 106

THE WORLD'S LONGEST WAR LASTED 680 YEARS

In contrast to the Anglo-Zanzibar war that lasted only 40 minutes, the Romans and the Persians were battling it out for nearly 700 years, making it the longest war in history. The war began in 54 BC and ended in 628 AD. The worst thing about the near 700 year conflict is that neither side won. All that remained to show for it was political and financial chaos on both sides. In reality, It's no surprise that the war lasted so long, since the Romans and the Persians were the two prominent empires of the first millennium. They had to both defend their territory or risk losing it.

THE ALBANIAN CAPITAL, TIRANA, DOESN'T HAVE A MCDONALD'S

This may sound like a rubbish fact, but it is actually the only capital in Europe that doesn't have one (other than the Vatican). It does, however, have a Burger King and a KFC. Although we don't know the exact reason for this, it is thought that the owners of 'Kolnat' (Albania's version of McDonald's) are quite friendly with the government and would do all they can to stop McDonald's from arriving in Albania. It is rumoured that they even pay the government to refuse McDonald's a trading licence, although this can't be confirmed. Interestingly, Macedonia and Iceland have recently discontinued their McDonald's franchises, but it is not known why.

THE BAGHEERA KIPLINKGI SPIDER IS THE ONLY ONE THAT IS VEGETARIAN

Most spider species are carnivores and live on a diet of insects. Some even prey on small mammals and birds. Although, in the 1800's, the Bagheera Kiplingi spider was noted for having a strange diet consisting mostly of plant material. The spider is native to Central America and lives exclusively on mimosaceae trees. The beltian bodies which grow on the tree make up the 90% of the spider's diet. It will very occasionally steal and eat ant larvae from passers by, but this is said to be rare. Interestingly, this spider also doesn't spin webs as most other spiders use webs as a way of catching their prey.

ELVIS PRESLEY NEVER WROTE A SINGLE SONG

For an artist so iconic and so famous, it's hard to believe that he never wrote any of the 600 songs that he recorded or performed. There were many people responsible for writing the king's chart-topping hits, including, Jerry Lieber and Mike Stoller, Aaron Schroeder, and Otis Blackwell. This list is by no means exhaustive, but these were the most influential and most important to Elvis's music career. Interestingly, Elvis was turned down after an audition to join a gospel quartet when he was 19 years old, but by this point he was already recording music.

Fact 110

POPE BENEDICT IX WAS THE YOUNGEST IN HISTORY

■ ■ ■ ■ ■ ■ ■ ■ ■ ■ ■ ■ ■ ■ ■ ■ ■ ■ ■ ı

He was also the only pope to take the job three times between 1032 and 1048. The age at which he first took the papacy is subject of debate. Some say he was only 11 or 12 years old, but other more verifiable sources suggest age 20. Either way, he was still the youngest pope ever. Interestingly, he was also one of the most scandalous popes in history. According to many sources he was renowned for "homosexual acts", and they spoke of his "rapes, murders, and other unspeakable acts of violence and sodomy". He was also accused by some of bestiality. One has to wonder whether it's all true?!

IKEA IS AN ACRONYM

The home furnishing giant is named after its founder, his family's farm, and his hometown. Ingvar Kamprad, Elmtaryd, Agunnaryd. Ingvar opened the first IKEA store in Almhult, Sweden, in 1958. Spreading quickly, stores were opened in Norway in 1963 and Denmark in 1968. Today, IKEA has stores in over 60 countries, with plans to expand further (mainly into South America and South East Asia). Interestingly, the largest store is currently in Manila in the Philippines, which is a whopping 65,000 square metres. To give you an idea of the sheer size, 10 Airbus A380's (the largest aircraft in the world) could fit into 64,000 square metres.

ONLY 9 PEOPLE WORKED ON THE NINTENDO 64 GAME, 'GOLDENEYE'

In comparison to today where there would be many more developers for a single console game, it took just 9 people to create Goldeneye. Arguably, Goldeneye was a game that was way ahead of its time in terms of graphics and playability. The company, 'Rare', also produced other games for Nintendo and gained a small stake in the company after releasing 'Donkey Kong Country' in 1994. Interestingly, Nintendo and Sony later worked together to create the PlayStation, which was to be a joint venture, although Nintendo pulled the plug when they realised Sony wanted the rights to the games. This forced Sony to find their own game developers, which didn't seem to work out too badly.

GPS COSTS $750 MILLION PER YEAR TO OPERATE

And yet it's free for everyone to use. How, you might ask?! Unknown to the US population, it is actually tax revenue that is used to pay for the infrastructure upkeep. GPS (global positioning system) was invented by the U.S. military in 1978 to track the exact location of its troops anywhere in the world. The system consists of 24 satellites in Earth orbit costing approximately $12 billion. The system became fully active in 1993. Interestingly, there are two levels of accuracy – the SPS (standard positioning system) available to all, and the PPS (precise positioning system) only available to the US military and its allies.

Fact 114

LAUGHTER IS GOOD FOR YOU

■■■■■■■■■■■■■■■■■■■■

Not only does it help keep you healthy, it also has the same effect on others. Laughing for 15 minutes per day can help weight loss, reduce stress, release endorphins (feel good hormones) and boost your immune system function. Laughing is also contagious - if someone is laughing, others are more likely to laugh too. Do not laugh deliberately though, as deliberate laughter can be a sign of mental health problems. So with all of these benefits, we should all be finding something we can have a good laugh at. Just be careful nobody around you is cherophobic.

THE STATE OF ALASKA HAS THE MOST SERIAL KILLERS IN THE U.S.

■■■■■■■■■■■■■■■■■■■■■

An interesting statistic, but one has to ask why this is the case. In Alaska, 1 in 65,000 people are likely to be victims of a violent attack. Alaska is a relatively sparse country in terms of population, and it is thought that this is one of the drivers behind the emergence of so many killers. It is very easy to dig a hole in a remote location in order to hide a body. Additionally, there aren't many other people, and killers will think that they can get away with such atrocities. Alaska also has pretty long, harsh winters, causing high rates of depression. This may also have an impact on peoples' mental stability.

Fact 116

DEEP SPACE IS FREEZING COLD, EVEN NEXT TO A STAR

■ ■ ■ ■ ■ ■ ■ ■ ■ ■ ■ ■ ■ ■ ■ ■ ■ ■ ｡

There are no particles in space, therefore nothing to vibrate and radiate energy. Temperature is a measure of particle vibration; so no particles - no temperature. So why is Mercury so hot? As the closest planet to the sun, it is made of solid particles and has a gaseous atmosphere (also made of particles). The thermal radiation from the sun travels through the vacuum of space as waves. When the waves arrive at Mercury 3.2 minutes later, they cause particles in the atmosphere and in the rock to vibrate, increasing their temperature. Although, the space in between is still absolute zero, even right next to the sun. That said, it's not advisable to go there, since you're also made of particles.

MICHAEL JACKSON'S MOST SUCCESSFUL YEAR WAS 2010

Michael Jackson was (and still is) the third highest-selling musical artist of all time. Despite already being successful, his record sales rocketed after his death on 25th June 2009, making 2010 the best year in his musical career. Jackson sold 35 million copies of his albums, bringing a revenue of $210 million that year alone. He remains the highest paid dead celebrity (closely followed by Elvis Presley) and still has over 30 million listeners per month on Spotify. Michael's Neverland Ranch is now owned by a family friend, Ronald Burkle, who bought the theme park for $22 million in 2020. Interestingly, the ranch's animals are now rehoused in various places across the U.S.

Fact 118

THE HIGHEST MOUNTAIN IN THE SOLAR SYSTEM IS 'OLYMPUS MONS' ON MARS

Although Mars is much smaller than Earth (0.6x), it is still home to a pretty impressive mountain. The highest of Earth's mountains, 'Everest', stands at 5.5 miles in height. 'Olympus Mons' on Mars stands at an impressive 16 miles high (three times bigger). The base of the mountain also covers an area as big as Arizona state. Interestingly, the air pressure at the top of mount Everest is still much higher than the surface of Mars, even though we can't breathe up there without additional support. The air pressure on the ground on Earth is 760 mmHg, the top of Everest is 253 mmHg, and the Martian surface only 4.6 mmHg.

ARGENTINA HAS THE DIRTIEST NATIONAL TEAM IN THE WORLD

In all football World Cups combined, Argentina have bagged more yellow and red cards than any other team. Regardless of the fact that Argentina produces some world class players, and arguably the best of all time (Lionel Messi), they still produce players that are a danger to both themselves and others. Famously, in the 1990 world Cup in Italy, they cheated their way to the final by diving and kicking other players. This style of play was branded the 'anti-football'. That year they were beaten by a dubiously awarded German penalty kick. Deserved? Maybe! Interestingly, this style of foul play isn't uncommon in the Argentinian football league.

JESUS WASN'T BORN ON 25TH DECEMBER

■■■■■■■■■■■■■■■■■■■■

We are all used to the idea that this is the birthday o
Jesus Christ. Although, this isn't actually true. Th
celebration of Christmas doesn't actually have anythin
to do with Jesus's birth. The earliest 'modern' Christmo
celebrations date back to 336 AD (after Jesus died).
was the Roman 'Emperor Constantine' who decided t
make December 25th a Christian celebration. This wo
supposedly done to 'weaken or overshadow' pagan c
other religious celebrations happening at the sam
time of year. Interestingly, some historians claim Jesu
was born in Spring, but there isn't much evidence fo
this, and we will likely never know the exact date o
even location of the birth.

Fact 121

THE FIRST DINOSAUR FOSSIL WAS ACKNOWLEDGED IN 1815

■ ı

Of course, dinosaur fossils have been unearthed many times throughout history, but ancient cultures passed them off as being mythical creatures, such as dragons or giant humans. The first of such bones to be properly studied was the femur from a Megalosaurus, found in 1676. Chemist, Robert Plot, recognised that it was too big to belong to any known animal. The real discovery came in 1815, when William Buckland, a student of geology at Oxford, found more fossils belonging to Megalosaurus. He later published the first scientific paper describing a non-flying lizard-like animal. The term 'dinosauria', meaning 'great- lizard' was coined by biologist, Sir Richard Owen, in 1841.

Fact 122

VOLKSWAGEN MAKES SAUSAGES AS WELL AS CARS

■ ■ ■ ■ ■ ■ ■ ■ ■ ■ ■ ■ ■ ■ ■ ■ ■ ■ ﹒

Not exactly something that the car giant is well known for, but it is true. Volkswagen started making food for its workers back in 1938 at the remote Wolfsburg plant. Where the plant is situated, there aren't many shops to buy lunch. As the rumour goes, their currywurst was so popular with the workers that they began to produce it commercially in 1973. The factory now produces around 20,000 sausages per day from locally sourced meat. There are also two different sizes of sausage (5 and 10 inches). Interestingly, beef was removed from the recipe following the 1990's BSE outbreak in the UK.

NEARLY HALF THE POPULATION OF UGANDA IS UNDER 15 YEARS OF AGE

An interesting statistic. The reason is due to the country's rapidly expanding population. Births outweigh deaths by a large margin, with each woman of fertile age having on average 6 children. At the current rate, Its population is predicted to rise from 35 million today to 105 million in 2050. This enormous increase is said to be due to very high fertility rates amongst both men and women. Interestingly, the country is poorly equipped economically to deal with such an increase, as most Ugandans still live in severe poverty. In contrast to high fertility rates in parts of Africa, fertility rates in the West are dropping alarmingly. The cause of this is still unknown.

MOST SOCIAL MEDIA PLATFORMS ARE BANNED IN CHINA

The big guns such as Facebook, Instagram, and Twitter, have all been banned by the Chinese Communist Party. Although, they aren't the only government to ban them; Iran, North Korea, and Russia also repeatedly try to ban their use (Facebook, particularly). The Chinese government operates a strict firewall system known as the 'Great Firewall', which blocks not only social media, but other businesses and websites that don't suit the country's interests. Thankfully, there are ways around this, such as using VPN's and proxy sites. Interestingly, TikTok is doing very well in China, as it was developed there. They also have a communication app called 'WeChat', similar to WhatsApp.

Fact 125

SNOW IN THE SAHARA DESERT IS MORE COMMON THAN YOU'D THINK

The most recent snowfall in the Sahara was in January 2022, but there have been many other episodes prior to this. The northern Sahara experiences low-pressure cyclones during the winter months, bringing in moist air from the Atlantic Ocean, Mediterranean Sea, and Indian Ocean. Rain is relatively common in the outer parts of the desert, and snow formation is also possible. However, the same cannot be said for the centre of the desert, which is an incredibly arid environment all year round (very little moisture) and temperatures can range from 25°F (-4°C) in the night to over 104°F (40°C) in the day.

Fact 126

TINA TURNER WAS THE FIRST FEMALE ON THE FRONT OF ROLLING STONE MAGAZINE

■■■■■■■■■■■■■■■■■■■

Hailed as the queen of rock n roll, Tina Turner appeared on the front cover of the second edition of 'Rolling Stone' on 25th November 1967. The magazine which still exists today, was created by Jann Wenner and Ralph Gleason from San Francisco, U.S. Rolling Stone is sold in more than 15 other countries around the world and even has a German version. Interestingly, Tina missed out only to a costumed John Lennon, who was featured on the front of the very first edition of the magazine on 9th November 1967. At this time, the band were celebrating the release of their new album, Sgt Pepper's Lonely Hearts Club Band.

NEUTRON STARS ARE THE MOST DENSE MATERIAL IN THE UNIVERSE

Who thinks they're hard? Not as hard as a neutron star! If you were to take a teaspoon of the material from a neutron star, it would have a mass of 90 million tonnes. It is also approximately 10 billion times stronger than steel. In order to create such a dense material it would require an incredible amount of force. Neutron stars are the remains of a star that ended its life as a supernova, where most of the matter has been expelled, leaving just a small dense ball of neutrons. The gravity is also large enough to disturb space-time. Like with velocity, time also slows with increasing gravity. The more massive an object is, the more gravity it has, and the slower time goes.

Fact 128

THE SIMPSONS CHARACTERS WERE INSPIRED BY THE CREATOR'S FAMILY

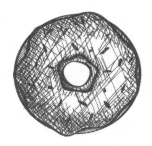

The creator of the Simpsons, Matt Groening, was born to Margaret Wiggum and Homer Groening. He also had two sisters. You guessed it – they were called Lisa and Maggie. In school, Matt was a talented cartoonist and comic sketch artist. After graduating college, he caught the eye of TV producer, Albert Brooks. Groening's work first appeared on 'The Tracey Ullman Show', in a short animated segment. He later teamed up with David Cohen and began working on the Simpsons. The duo were also responsible for creating the acclaimed 'Fururama' in 1997.

ANDRE THE GIANT ONCE TOOK A NAP DURING A WRESTLING MATCH

Nobody is 100% sure if this fact is true, but it's funny nevertheless. During a match with 'Big John Studd' in the 1980's, The giant allegedly took a nap whilst being held in an 8 minute long face lock. Strangely enough, this is the only notable action of the match. Needless to say it wasn't the most enthralling of matches, especially for Andre it seems. He reportedly had his eyes closed for a time during the match, but was definitely not unconscious. The face lock by Studd was also purported to be the longest in wrestling history.

HARRY STYLES HAS 4 NIPPLES

A titillating fact for some. The 'One Direction' star confirmed this to be true in an interview with Chelsea Handler in 2017. Apparently Harry wasn't at all coy about admitting it, and went on to explain that there are two 'normal' nipples in the right place, and two additional nipples further down the chest. These additional nipples are said to be called 'supernumerary nipples'. The condition which brings about this feature is called 'polythelia' and is apparently more common than one would imagine. It is estimated that 1-5% of the population actually have supernumerary nipples. It is also said to be genetic.

YOU COULD CELEBRATE THE NEW YEAR TWICE IN THE SAME YEAR

Well, technically three times if you celebrate Chinese new year. However, sticking to Western culture, it is possible to celebrate new year twice and also have a little time to recover in between. If you reside in a country such as New Zealand, who are one of the first to celebrate the new year, it is possible to then fly to Hawaii across the international date line to celebrate it again 23 hours later. Because Hawaii is one of the last to celebrate the new year, you can comfortably fit in a 10 hour flight, plus a reasonable nap at the other end. Interestingly, this is the only way that you can effectively 'time travel' whilst staying on Earth.

Fact 132

THERE IS NO SCIENTIFIC PAPER PROVING THAT HIV INFECTION CAUSES AIDS

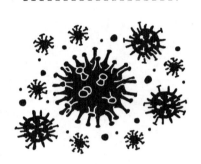

This is something we all just take for granted, because we are told so. Before we explore, it is important to know that HIV is a virus that is said to destroy cells in the immune system. AIDS is a condition you acquire when you don't have enough immune cells left to fight infection. But are the two interlinked as strongly as doctors would have us believe? Well, not exactly. In the absence of direct proof, there is certainly correlation between the two. But, correlation doesn't always mean causation. There are still many other factors at play in most AIDS cases (drug use and malnutrition), despite a person's HIV status. Additionally, many healthy people with HIV never develop AIDS.

THERE ARE ONLY 5 COUNTRIES IN THE WORLD ENDING WITH THE LETTER 'L'

A completely useless fact by all accounts, however this one is really good for a bit of pub trivia with your friends or family. Interestingly, none of them are in the same continent, unless you would class Israel as Europe?! So the first one you already have. The other four are Portugal, Brazil, Nepal, and Senegal. It is interesting to see how fast your friends can name them all. This is one of those that can be incredibly frustrating.

BLACK ISN'T ACTUALLY A COLOUR

When we see every other colour (apart from black), our eyes are registering the frequencies of light waves that enter the cone cells of the retina. They will then transmit a signal that our brain will register as a certain colour. However, when we see black, we're not actually seeing anything at all. The brain registers black when there is a complete lack of light entering the eye. This is why darkness is black (makes sense, right?!). Interestingly, humans all see colours slightly differently. How do you know that the red you see, is the red somebody else sees?! Makes little difference anyway, as you have both been told it's red, even if they are slightly different colours.

RUSSIA HAS 11 TIME ZONES

....

Being the largest country in the world, and spanning half the width of the Northern hemisphere, you would probably expect such a statistic. Although there are some subtleties here that we need to understand. Moscow, in the West, is in the same time zone as Nairobi in Kenya. Anadyr, in the far East, has the same time zone as the Marshall Islands in the Pacific Ocean. The distance between Moscow and Anadyr is only 3,500 nautical miles, whereas Nairobi to the Marshall Islands is 8,000 nautical miles. We have the curvature of the Earth to thank for the huge difference. In addition, Russia only has 11 time zones due to the more Western, Kaliningrad province, nestled between Poland and Lithuania.

EATING BIRTHDAY CAKE IS AN ANCIENT TRADITION

The tradition of eating birthday cake can be traced back as far as ancient Egypt, although they also only celebrated the birthday of their gods, not ordinary people as we do today. The ancient Greeks then adopted the idea of birthday cake. They would also gather many people together and make lots of noise in order to scare away evil spirits (birthday parties). People still make lots of noise today, but not to scare away spirits; rather consume them. The modern birthday cake originated in Germany in the middle ages. Children would receive a cake containing a candle for every year of life. The celebration was known as 'kinderfest' and was more similar to the way we celebrate today.

MOST MODERN GAME CONSOLES ARE SOLD AT A LOSS

On release, both the PS3 and the Xbox 360 were sold at a loss to their respective companies. Apparently it is not uncommon for game console companies to do this and there is a good reason. Console games and additional parts are much cheaper to produce than the console unit itself, and companies who produce the consoles will bank on the fact that they will make up the losses on the future sale of such products. Interestingly, the PS3 makes a larger loss ($300 per unit) than the Xbox 360 ($130 per unit). This may be one of the reasons Nintendo pulled the plug on the PlayStation deal. Without access to the game royalties, their losses would be substantial.

Fact 138

YOU USED TO BE CONSIDERED AN IDIOT IF YOU SMILED IN A PHOTOGRAPH

■■■■■■■■■■■■■■■■■■■■

If you've ever looked at an old family photo album, you may notice that people appear more and more miserable the further back you go. Although, this has nothing to do with happiness. In the Victorian era smiling in a photograph was considered idiotic behaviour. Even wedding photographs didn't show people smiling. Luckily today things are different. Photographers encourage participants to smile to show they are having fun. "Say cheese!!" A request we now hear quite often. Saying the word 'cheese' creates a smile shape with the mouth giving the illusion of happiness, even when people have an aversion to photographs.

THE EARTH'S SPIN IS SLOWING DOWN

The Earth's rotation has been slowing down ever since the collision that formed the moon 4.5 billion years ago. The moon's gravity pulls on the Earth, acting as a brake and causing its spin to slow. Although, this is no big event. The slowing of the spin only adds approximately 2 milliseconds (less than a jiffy) onto a day each century. But, what will happen when it eventually stops spinning? Well, the Earth will experience a 6 month day, followed by a 6 month night. In addition, the Earth will be so unstable that it may even tip over, exposing the poles to direct sunlight. As well as uncertain temperatures and no seasons, the world will certainly be a lot wetter.

AFTER CHILDHOOD, YOU NO LONGER NEED YOUR TONSILS

■ ■ ■ ■ ■ ■ ■ ■ ■ ■ ■ ■ ■ ■ ■ ■ ■ ■ ı

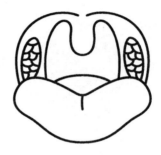

According to Giulia Enders, the author of the book 'Gut', your tonsils are incredibly important to you, but only as a child. During childhood, they are used to assess the type of pathogens (infectious agents) that are likely to enter the body through the mouth. Once they detect these pathogens, they produce antibodies, which will remain with you for many years. It also gives the immune system a head start if you accidentally ingest something dangerous. However, between ages 7 and 10 their job is pretty much done. They have gathered all of the information your immune system needs. As your immune system 'jumps ship', your tonsils are just left there and may become prone to infection.

MONOPOLY IS THE HIGHEST SELLING BOARD GAME OF ALL TIME

It is estimated that up to one billion people worldwide have been lucky enough to play Monopoly. An early version of the popular landlord game was designed and patented by a lady named Lizzie Magie in 1904. Following release, others tweaked and made their own variations of the game at home. The most notable version was that by the American, Charles Darrow, in 1934. He presented the 'tweaked' game to Parker Brothers in 1935, who originally rejected the idea. Luckily, since changing their mind, over 200 million copies of the modern Monopoly game have been sold. Interestingly, Darrow's version of the Monopoly man was modelled on J.P. Morgan.

THE MANAGER OF GUINNESS STARTED THE GUINNESS BOOK OF RECORDS

The Guinness book of records also holds a record for being the best-selling copyright book of all time. The idea for a world record book came from Sir Hugh Beaver, the managing director of Guinness from 1946 to 1960. He attended a shooting party in Wexford county, Ireland, in 1951, where he missed a shot at a golden plover. After missing, he was embroiled in a heated discussion about which game bird was the fastest, the golden plover or a red grouse. Annoyed that there was no data on the subject, he thought a book settling such debates would be a good idea. The first 'Guinness Book of Records' was released in 1955, but with no mention of the fastest game bird.

THERE IS A TYPE OF LIQUID THAT HUMANS CAN BREATHE

■ ■ ■ ■ ■ ■ ■ ■ ■ ■ ■ ■ ■ ■ ■ ■ ■ ■ ₁

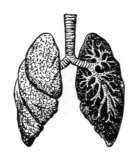

Perfluorohexane is a fluorine-based solvent that is biologically inert (doesn't affect cells) and chemically stable. Although the name suggests it may be poisonous, it can actually be breathed in liquid state and still sustain life. Perfluorohexane has the capability to dissolve oxygen at much higher concentrations than other liquids (like water, or blood). Because of this high concentration, oxygen is pushed into the blood in the same amounts as it would be in air upon breathing. In the 1990's, perfluorohexane was used in experimental treatments of patients who had experienced internal lung burns, although it was found not to improve outcomes.

THE BIBLE HAS BEEN TRANSLATED INTO FICTIONAL LANGUAGES

■■■■■■■■■■■■■■■■■■■

It's certainly debatable how useful such a translation would be, unless of course we all decide to adopt 'Klingon' (or another) as our native language. There have been various projects to translate parts of the bible into the following languages: Klingon (Star Trek), Quenya (Tolkien), Na'vi (Avatar), Láadan (Native Tongue, Suzette Haden Elgin), and LOLcat (internet slang). Most of the above translations have been part of collaborative projects, allowing the public to make contributions to parts of the text. As of 2008, 61% of the bible had already been translated into LOLcat, although there is no current information on its progress.

CANCER DOESN'T FIT INTO ANY DISEASE CLASSIFICATION

As far as diseases go, cancer is a strange one. Medical scientists have tried for many years to uncover a pathological process common to all cancers, but this has proved notoriously difficult. When we talk about causation, most human diseases fit into one of the following categories: deficiency disease (dietary), genetic disease (hereditary), or communicable disease (bacteria/viruses). Cancer is none of these directly. You could put cancer into a somewhat sketchy 'physiological disease' class; but if we're being pedantic, most physiological diseases (diseases of cells) are also caused by one of the above factors, particularly poor diet.

IF YOU SQUARE A NUMBER WITH ALL 1'S YOUR ANSWERS WILL BE PALINDROMIC

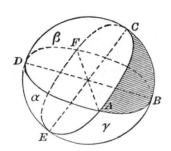

For those who don't know what 'palindrome' means, it is something that reads the same backwards as it does forwards. So, let's have a look at the maths. We will ignore 1 x 1, as the answer is only one number. But 11 is where things get interesting. 11 x 11 = 121. 111 x 111 = 12,321. 1,111 x 1,111 = 1,234,321. You get the idea. 11,111 has five ones, meaning that 5 will be the highest number in the answer. You guessed it, 123,454,321. But what happens when you get to 10? Try it out...

DENTISTRY IS THE OLDEST MEDICAL PROFESSION, DATING BACK TO 7,000 BC

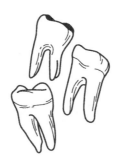

The peoples of the Indus Valley (modern day Pakistan) were said to be the first to perform dentistry as much as 9,000 years ago, making it one of the oldest medical professions. Artefacts have been found in the valley, including bow drills, which were said to have been crafted by bead workers. The intention of the bow drills was allegedly to cure tooth ailments. Despite this ancient practice, 'The Little Medicinal Book for All Kinds of Diseases and Infirmities of the Teeth' (1530) was the very first book dedicated solely to dentistry. It wasn't until 1723 that Pierre Fauchard (the father of dentistry) wrote the first comprehensive book on how to care for and treat teeth.

THE PIONEER OF PRINGLES WAS BURIED IN A PRINGLES TUBE

In 1966, the Procter & Gamble employee 'Fredric Baur' found a way to stack potato chips on top of each other in a uniform way, instead of throwing them in a bag. Following the momentous achievement, he seemingly joked to his family that he wanted to be buried in a Pringles tube. His family later realised that this will was no joke. After he died in 2008, Fredric's eldest son, Larry, honoured his father's wish and placed part of his ashes inside a Pringles tube before burying them at a cemetery in Springfield, US. If you're wondering what flavour it was, it was the 'original' red Pringles. What flavour tube would you be buried in?

Fact 149

MINERAL WATER AND SPRING WATER ARE THE SAME, BUT DIFFERENT

■■■■■■■■■■■■■■■■■■■■■

A confusing fact? Mineral and spring water both come from an underground source, which is geologically and physically protected. In both cases, water flows naturally to the surface and contains dissolved minerals. The differences, however, lie in both the mineral composition and regulation. The mineral profile of mineral water must be constant over time, whereas that of spring water may change. This must be measured regularly to ensure stability. Mineral water is also recognised and heavily regulated by local authorities in order to ensure purity and prevent contamination. Spring water doesn't have such strict controls.

THERE WAS A RUMOURED SHORTAGE OF NINJAS IN JAPAN

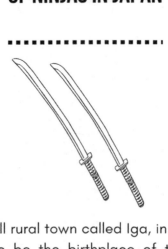

There is a small rural town called Iga, in central Japan, that is said to be the birthplace of the ninja. In a recent 'Planet Money' podcast, Sally Herships visited the town and reported a shortage of ninjas and ninja performers. She also reported that new ninjas in Iga can earn up to $85,000. The week following the podcast, Iga had 114 enquiries from across the world, asking about ninja vacancies. The highest number of enquiries being from Spain (16). The mayor of Iga, Sakae Okamoto, responded to the podcast stating that there was no shortage of ninjas and that the salary quoted by Herships was "unrealistic, and that ninjas cannot earn that much".

Fact 151

MCDONALD'S SELLS SPAGHETTI IN THE PHILIPPINES

■■■■■■■■■■■■■■■■■■■■

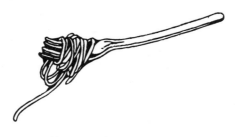

Believe it or not, McSpaghetti used to be a staple part of the McDonald's menu worldwide, although it was discontinued in the 1980's due to lack of demand. There are, however, two places in the world where you can still purchase a McSpaghetti – the Philippines and Orlando, Florida. Its popularity in the Philippines is unrivalled and will remain a staple part of their McDonald's menu for years to come. Interestingly, the McDonalds on International Drive, Orlando, is somewhat of a novelty. As the biggest Mc Donald's in the world, it also serves other specialty items such as pizza, omelette, waffles and cheesesteaks.

1912 WAS THE LAST OLYMPICS TO HAVE FULLY GOLD MEDALS

This fact is in the Guinness book of world records. The first Olympic gold medals were awarded in 1904, prior to which only silver and bronze medals existed (from 1896 onward). Fully gold medals were only given to Olympians in 1904, 1908, and 1912. As a result of the first world war, the use of gold declined in 1914, and the 'gold standard' all but collapsed. Gold medals today are made mostly of silver, but are plated with a layer of gold weighing 6 grams. The medals are also larger than the original gold version. Interestingly, gold remains one of the best long-term investments someone can have due to its stability in the markets. Many places in the world still hold gold reserves.

COLD SHOWERS HAVE MANY HEALTH BENEFITS

You might want to learn a few Wim Hof breathing techniques before diving into a cold shower. Although they may not feel too pleasant, they can have many benefits for the body and mind. Such benefits include: improved circulation, improved immune function, soothed muscles, faster weight loss, healthy looking hair, reduction in anxiety and depression, and making you feel more alert. Quite an impressive list, although that's not to say that a hot shower doesn't have its merits too, particularly if you want to get rid of skin blemishes.

Fact 154

THE HIGHEST NON-FATAL FALL WAS 10,160 METRES (6.31 MILES)

■ ■ ■ ■ ■ ■ ■ ■ ■ ■ ■ ■ ■ ■ ■ ■ ■ ■ ■ ı

A remarkable story. The Yugoslavian flight attendant, Vesna Vulović, was the only survivor of a JAT airlines D-C9 crash on 26th January 1972. The plane was on its way from Stockholm in Sweden to Belgrade in Serbia when the fuselage exploded into three pieces. Luckily, Vesna was in the rear section of the plane where she was held in by a food trolley. She passed out shortly after the explosion, which protected her heart from the impact. Her section of the plane also landed in heavy Czech snow, which cushioned the impact. Vesna was in a coma for days, suffered many broken bones, and was temporarily paralysed. Although she did make a full recovery and was able to walk again after 10 months.

THE SOUND OF A LIGHTSABER WAS MADE FROM TWO DIFFERENT SOUNDS

■■■■■■■■■■■■■■■■■■■

Arguably one of the most iconic sounds in movie history. The only objects that creator 'Ben Burtt' used to create the lightsaber was an idling 35 mm projector and a buzzing 1970's tube TV. Although the lightsaber is a fictional weapon, it has inspired many people to try to create a real version. The first person to do so was a Russian YouTuber named 'Alex Burkan', who has also earned a place in the Guinness book of records for his trouble. To create it, he used a modified hydrogen/oxygen burner from a motorcycle. Although a working prototype, it does need many improvements before it becomes the finished product. The current version only works for 30 seconds before burning out.

GRAPEFRUIT AFFECTS THE ACTIVITY OF 43 DIFFERENT MEDICINES

■■■■■■■■■■■■■■■■■■■

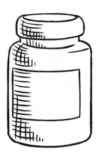

Due to improvements in medical care, many people may now have to forgo a refreshing glass of grapefruit juice with breakfast. Most medicines for common ailments such as high cholesterol, high blood pressure, allergies, and many more, are affected by one of the chemicals present in grapefruit juice. CYP3A4 is an important enzyme in the liver and digestive tract which is responsible for the breakdown of such medicines, ensuring that they remain in the blood in the correct concentrations. Grapefruit is a potent inhibitor of CYP3A4, meaning there could be complications if grapefruit is taken at the same time as these medications.

OPERATING THEATRES USED TO HAVE A LIVE AUDIENCE

Indeed this is the very reason they are called operating 'theatres'. As far back as the 16th century, doctors used to perform anatomical displays for eager onlookers, using the cadavers of deceased prisoners. Although, at this point, no patients were alive during surgery. It was merely a way for people to pay to either learn anatomy, or simply just be entertained. The operations were quite a spectacle and live music would often accompany the dissections. By the early 19th century, live patients were also being operated on in public. Although, as surgery slowed due to anaesthetics, the public largely lost interest. Doctors also began to realise that having audiences increased the risk of infection.

Fact 158

THE TATTOO GUN WAS INSPIRED BY THOMAS EDISON

■■■■■■■■■■■■■■■■■■■

We've all heard of Thomas Edison, who was famed for inventing the incandescent light bulb (although this isn't strictly true). He was also the brains behind the electric pen, which would eventually become the first tattoo 'gun'. When Edison invented the electric pen in 1876, it was originally intended as a text duplication device. The subsequent designs for its modification were patented by the New York tattoo artist 'Samuel O'Reilly' in 1891. Before the modification of Edison's pen, tattoo artists were already experimenting with other machines that delivered ink to the skin. Eventually O'Reilly's design won out, and became the most commonly used tattooing device.

A HANGOVER IS A VALID REASON TO BE OFF WORK

Well, only if you work for 'Dice', a UK live music ticketing app. The company is based in Shoreditch, London, and they allow their employees up to 4 'hangover sick days' per year. As the business is heavily invested in live music, they encourage staff to attend many live music events around the city. If staff happen to drink a little too much during an event, the company doesn't judge them too harshly and will allow them to take a 'duvet day'. If staff are struggling, all they must do is send their boss three emojis in the staff WhatsApp group: music, beer, and sick.

JULIUS CAESAR'S SON WAS CALLED CAESARION

Despite the name, I can say with certainty that he was born naturally to his mother, Cleopatra, in 47 BC. The only deliberation was whether Caesarion was actually the son of Julius Caesar, as it wasn't confirmed by the Emperor himself until a year after the boy's birth. Classical authors of the time cast doubts over Caesar's paternity. Interestingly, Caesarion only lived 17 years. During an affair with Cleopatra, Mark Anthony endeavoured to protect her (and the Caesar lineage), but subsequently lost a battle against Octavian in 31 BC. Caesarion was then executed by Octavian (soon to be 'Emperor Augustus') in 30 BC, changing the very trajectory of the Roman Empire.

THE QUIETEST ROOM IN THE WORLD IS IN MINNESOTA

he anechoic chamber at the 'Orfield Labs' in Minnesota is the quietest place in the world, measuring 9.4 dB (decibels). To give a comparison, a very quiet bedroom at night registers approximately 30 db. The chamber walls are made from an outer 12 inches of concrete, double insulated steel, and large inner fibreglass wedges. The room is said to be 99.9% sound absorbent. In fact, so absorbent of external sounds, that a person in the room can hear their own heartbeat, breathing, and sometimes digestion. Companies tend to use the room to measure the loudness of devices, such as mobile phones, heart valves, CPAP machines, and more...

2015 WAS THE BEST YEAR IN HISTORY FOR THE FILM INDUSTRY

2015 gave birth to four of the highest-grossing films of all time. The films responsible were 'Jurassic world', 'Star Wars: The Force Awakens', 'Avengers: Age of Ultron', and 'Furious 7'. The leader of the pack, 'Star Wars: The Force Awakens' grossed over $2 billion, and was only the fourth film ever to do so. It also broke the record for the number of pre-release tickets sold, making $529 million in the opening weekend alone. This record was originally broken by 'Jurassic World' released just a few months earlier, grossing $524.4 million in its opening weekend. Talk about tight competition. 'Furious 7' also became the fastest film ever to gross $1 billion worldwide.

PAPUA NEW GUINEA HAS OVER 800 DIFFERENT LANGUAGES

Papua New Guinea is the most linguistically diverse place on the planet. Over 80% of its 8.1 million people reside in rural areas, where contact with the modern world, or even other tribes, is limited. Due to isolation, most ancient tribal languages have persisted until today. There are said to be 852 living languages, although 12 of them now have no living speakers left. Luckily, one of the official languages in the country is English and most people have at least a basic knowledge. It is also the political language and the language of school instruction. Although, 'Enga' and 'Huli' are the two most widely spoken local languages.

Fact 164

ONE HORSE HAS APPROXIMATELY
15 HORSEPOWER

■■■■■■■■■■■■■■■■■■■■

As the name suggests, the power output of motors was compared to that of draft horses. The term was coined in the late 18th century by James Watt, a Scottish scientist with an interest in both the energy usage and power output of steam engines. As you may have guessed, the 'Watt' unit of power was also named after him. Mechanical 'horsepower' is 735.5 Watts – that's the power needed to raise a 75 kg mass by one metre, in one second. Most motors are now measured against this standard of power output. Interestingly, upon testing a horse for its mechanical 'horsepower', the animal is able to produce 11,032.5 Watts of power, which is 15hp. How did this happen?!

Fact 165

THE TOOTH FAIRY IS NEARLY 1,000 YEARS OLD

It is thought that the tooth fairy story originated in the Norse regions of Europe in the 10th Century. A 'tand-fe' or 'tooth fee' is referred to in some of the earliest literary works of Northern Europe. As written in the 'Edda', adults would pay children a small fee when their first tooth came out. At this time, a child's teeth were said to bring good luck, and many would wear necklaces fashioned from multiple teeth to bring them luck in battle. The modern tooth fairy was introduced much later, with its first mention in the Chicago Tribune in 1908. The writer encouraged parents to tell their children the story of a 'fairy' who would leave 5 cents under their pillow for every loose tooth that was pulled by the dentist.

PORT WINE WAS AN ACCIDENT

■ ı

French wine imports were cut off from the British during the maritime war that began in 1689, meaning Britain had to look elsewhere to satisfy their cravings. As British businessmen settled in the Porto region of Northern Portugal, they began to discover the vineyards of the 'Douro' region. Although delightful, transportation of Portuguese wine to the UK often took a long time, which led to preservation issues. To counter the problem, the British fortified the wine with grape brandy, which allowed it to survive the journey. Due to the sweetness, the British were rather fond of the new creation and would often forgo the planned additional fermentation stages back in the UK.

THE FIRST PRIMARK STORE OPENED IN 1969

The first store was opened under the name of 'Penney's' in June 1969. The company still trades under his name in Ireland. The first store was opened by the then chairman, Arthur Ryan, on behalf of the Weston amily. The Weston family (a family of Canadian business people) and its holdings own over 200 companies worldwide, including Penneys/Primark. The Weston's focus mostly on stores retailing food, legal drugs, and fashion. The UK currently has 191 Primark stores (at the time of writing), making the UK its largest market. Despite rumours, Primark joined the Ethical Trading Initiative (ETI) in 2006, helping to respect the rights of workers worldwide.

Fact 168

THE PILOT'S KIDS CAUSED THE AEROFLOT 593 CRASH

■■■■■■■■■■■■■■■■■■■

The Russian airline's flight was on its way from Moscow to Hong Kong when it crashed into the Kuznetsk Alatau mountain range in Southern Russia. Upon investigation there was no evidence of malfunctions, but something else very strange did happen. The flight recorder tracked the voices of the relief captain's son and daughter both in the cockpit. Without the pilot knowing, his 15 year-old son had turned off the autopilot function for the plane's ailerons (for steering) causing the other functions to also disengage. This caused the plane to nose-dive and despite attempts by the first-officer to correct the plane, it crashed into the mountains killing all 75 passengers and 8 crew.

HARRY POTTER WAS REJECTED BY 12 PUBLISHERS

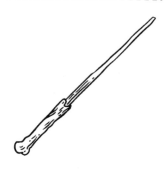

Although there appears to be no information available online about exactly which publishers rejected the first Harry Potter novel, the reason for rejection seemed somewhat general. The book was either too old-fashioned, too strange, too long, or too conventional. Despite having so many knock-backs, Joanne Kathleen Rowling pressed on, and eventually 'Harry Potter and The Philosopher's Stone' was published by Bloomsbury on 26th June 1997. If you are interested in reading the original pitch to the publishers, it is available to view online though many websites. Interestingly, Joanne is the UK's highest-selling living author and has a net worth of £820 million (at the time of writing).

THE UK AND PORTUGAL HAVE THE WORLD'S OLDEST ALLIANCE

The alliance between the two countries began back in 1147 when British crusaders helped the Portuguese king, Alonso I, capture Lisbon. However, the alliance wasn't made official until the 'Treaty of Windsor' was drawn up in 1386. The two countries have supplied military support to each other on numerous occasions over the years - against Napoleon in the early 19th century on the Iberian peninsula, and in both world wars in the 20th century. The two countries have never fought on opposite sides and also provide refuge for each other's citizens in the event of upheaval. The alliance holds strong even today.

Fact 171

THE LEANING TOWER OF PISA HAS SURVIVED MANY EARTHQUAKES

The earthquakes are not why the tower is leaning, but the reason it's leaning is also the reason why it survived the earthquakes. Confused? The leaning tower of Pisa was mistakenly built on soft sub-soil which lays beneath its 3m deep foundations. As it began to tilt, architects built additional floors with one side shorter than the other in order to correct the centre of gravity. This is why the tower has not yet fallen. Remarkably, when earthquakes have hit the city, the soft sub-soil acted like a shock absorber, preventing the tower from falling. What do you think? Will the tower eventually fall?

Fact 172

'SANTA'S SHORTCUT' HAS CUT FLIGHT TIMES

■■■■■■■■■■■■■■■■■■■■

A recent development in aviation is that planes are finally allowed to fly over the North pole and some of Antarctica. Originally, commercial flights were not allowed to be more than 3 hours from the nearest airfield, but that has now increased to 5 hours and 30 minutes. Such an increase gives planes enough time to transit the North pole and some of the Antarctic continent. Direct Flights from The US and UK to the South Pacific islands now come in at between 15 and 19 hours (as opposed to days, with a layover). Aircraft do, however, need to meet certain criteria and have additional equipment on board in order to fly the route. Staff also have to undergo additional training.

Fact 173

2-4% OF MAURITANIANS STILL LIVE AS SLAVES

The endemic problem of slavery in Mauritania dates back to the historical slave raids on Sub-Saharan Africa during the 17th and 18th centuries. Islamic slaves were taken and distributed to ports along the West and North African coast (as well as Europe and Arabia). Even today, slavery amongst these populations living in Mauritania is familial. Children will work as slaves for the same families their parents worked for. It is said that they know little of life outside of slavery and even questioning the idea of slavery is akin to questioning Islam itself. Mauritania was the last country to abolish slavery in 1981, although there were no laws passed to enforce it until 2007.

173

A STARFISH HAS NO BLOOD

■■■■■■■■■■■■■■■■■■■

They also have no brain, which is equally as interesting Starfish do have organs, and are definitely alive so need to keep their organs healthy. They do this by pumping sea water around their bodies. The water will supply essential nutrients, which can diffuse into cells from the vascular system. They also don't need a heart to do this. Interestingly, jellyfish, sponges, and corals also use seawater in a similar way. Starfish and others in the same class do have a nervous system, allowing them to respond to stimuli, but with no central control area (brain) allowing them to think 'freely'. Although difficult to prove, it is thought by some scientists that such animals can also feel pain.

INDIA IS HOME TO THE WORLD'S LARGEST STADIUM

Cricket is India's prize sport, so why not build the largest stadium in the world to celebrate it. The 'Narendra Modi Stadium' in Ahmedabad, India, has a capacity of 132,000. For comparison, this is 32,500 more than the 'Camp Nou', football stadium in Barcelona. Interestingly, the largest purpose built football stadium in the world is the 'Rungrado 1st May Stadium' in Pyongyang, North Korea, with a capacity of 114,000. This is worth a mention, as no football (soccer) is played at Narendra Modi, although it does feature many indoor football pitches. Most of the other 100,000+ capacity stadiums in the world are in North America and are home to the American Football teams.

THE THREE-POINT SEATBELT WAS INVENTED BY VOLVO

The first car to be sold with a three-point seatbelt was a Volvo PV544 back in 1959. This makes the design 64 years old (at the time of writing). Unlike most companies that like to monetise their patents, Volvo were so passionate about motoring safety that they allowed anyone to use the design free of charge. They also still allow other companies to access their car safety data. The three-point belt was a novel design, as it allowed a crash force to be spread over a larger area than a standard two-point belt, greatly reducing injuries. It also further restricts movement of the person during a collision. Interestingly, seat belts weren't made mandatory in the US and UK until much later.

BEES HAVE KNEES

Of course, this fact is going to be 'the bees knees'. The phrase comes from the fact that bees possess tiny pockets on their knees, in which to accumulate pollen. The more pollen a bee carries, the wealthier (in bee world) the animal is, since they use pollen to make honey. Interestingly, the bee population of the world is decreasing, which is somewhat alarming. There certainly will not 'bee' a doomsday prognosis for the world, as many think, but biodiversity would certainly suffer and we will need to find new ways to pollinate plants which are reliant on bees and other insects for survival. Some scientists are currently researching the use of tiny pollinating robots for this purpose.

Fact 178

FOR FIVE YEARS, THE DICTIONARY HAD A WORD THAT DIDN'T EXIST

■■■■■■■■■■■■■■■■■■■■■

Between 1934 and 1939, the word 'dord' was present in the Merriam-Webster dictionary. The word doesn't have any meaning, but was listed as a synonym of 'density', a term used in physics and chemistry. So, how did the error happen? Dictionaries have always listed words that can be abbreviated with a single letter, for example: 'D or d' can be used to abbreviate the word 'density'. 'D or d', when written on paper, can also be misinterpreted as a single word. As the story goes, the original paper from the dictionary's chemistry editor was lost and had to be retyped, which was the supposed reason for the error. The mistake was later noticed by an editor who found that 'dord' didn't seem to have an etymology.

178

Fact 179

THE MONA LISA WAS STOLEN FROM THE LOUVRE IN 1911

On 21st August, an Italian man named Vincenzo Peruggia pulled off the most memorable of crimes. After moving to Paris in 1908, Vincenzo got a job as a handyman at the Louvre and was responsible for installing glass casings around paintings. Ironically, such casings were installed to protect paintings and other artworks from theft. Due to being able to roam freely after closing time, Vincenzo was allowed ample time to steal the painting. Interestingly, he wasn't caught until 2 years after the painting was stolen. The police even arrested Pablo Picasso for the crime. Due to the media storm that followed the event, the empty wall also attracted many additional visitors to Paris.

THERE IS AN INSURANCE POLICY THAT COVERS ALIEN ABDUCTION

'Lloyds of London' and the 'St Lawrence Agency' in Florida are two companies offering such a policy. In order to make a claim, 'victims' must be prepared to provide details of the aliens, where they're from, and what type of spacecraft they use. In addition they must also pass a lie detector test and provide a signature from the leading alien, verifying the abduction. If it is possible to provide video footage or a witness statement, this is also beneficial. Both policies will cover up to $10 million in damages, covering both medical treatment and 'sarcasm' (in case a family member causes psychological trauma by not believing you).

Fact 181

OVER 2 MILLION CHINESE PEOPLE LIVE IN NUCLEAR BUNKERS

During the cold war in the 1960's and 70's, China became somewhat anxious about the prospect of nuclear war. As a result, the Mao government instructed workers to build bunkers under every city, capable of withstanding a nuclear blast. Beijing built over 10,000 bunkers during this time. When the cold war ended, the bunkers were leased to private investors who converted them to tiny residential units. Due to living conditions, the Chinese government does not want these areas documented. In 2015, Italian photographer, Antonio Faccilongo, had a visit request denied by Beijing's local council and was repeatedly turned away by security staff.

Fact 182

METALLICA WERE THE FIRST BAND TO PERFORM ON EVERY CONTINENT

■■■■■■■■■■■■■■■■■■■ı

"Sad but True!" By 2013, Metallica had become the only band to perform on all 7 continents in a single year. They also have a Guinness world record to prove it. The most spectacular of shows, named 'Freeze em All' took place in Antarctica on 8th December 2013. The gig was sponsored by Coca Cola and attendees were a variety of competition winners from central and South America. The winners got to go on a cruise around Antarctica and also attended the gig. The performance was done a little differently due to lack of electrical power and each fan was given a set of headphones, akin to a 'silent disco'. If you want to watch the record-breaking gig, it is available on YouTube.

EXTREME IRONING IS A SPORT

As the name suggests, people take their irons and ironing boards to remote locations and iron as many clothes as possible. The 'sport' originated in Leicester, UK, and was pioneered by Phil Shaw, a knitwear factory worker with a love for rock climbing. Unenthused by the amount of chores that awaited him at home after a hard day's work, he decided to take his ironing rock climbing with him. So pleased by his new extreme sport, he even embarked on a world tour to promote it back in 1999. After a documentary in 2003, the sport gained substantial attention, as it followed GB to a gold medal in the first ever 'Extreme Ironing World Championships' in Germany.

Fact 184

ANTIMATTER IS THE MOST EXPENSIVE MATERIAL ON EARTH

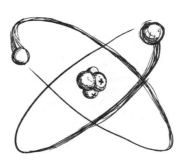

You may be wondering what on Earth antimatter is! For ease, it is the inverse of matter. Matter is made up of atoms containing protons(+), neutrons and electrons(-), whereas antimatter is made up of atoms containing antiprotons (-), antineutrons, and positrons (+ electrons). Interestingly, if you allow matter and antimatter to mix, because of the opposing charges they will cancel each other out, releasing incredible amounts of energy in the process. This makes antimatter incredibly destructive, and only 1g of it could produce an explosion similar to that of a nuclear bomb. If you wanted to lay your hands on 1g, it would likely cost you $62.5 trillion, as it has to be produced in a physics lab.

THE TERM 'RIDING SHOTGUN' COMES FROM THE WILD WEST

We've all 'called shotgun' at some point when we wanted the privilege of riding in the front passenger seat of the car. Although, there's a good chance that many people who use the phrase have no idea where it came from. The American 'old West' could be a hostile place and people who travelled from place to place in horse-drawn carriage would sometimes be held up and robbed at gunpoint. In order to deter such horrific acts, carriage drivers would have someone sit next to them with a weapon (usually a shotgun) and ward off potential attackers. This idea slowly worked its way into pop culture and even appeared in movies, which is probably why we use the phrase today.

Fact 186

THERE IS A WORLDWIDE SHORTAGE OF CRANES

Currently, a quarter of the world's cranes are set up in the UAE. It is estimated that the wait time for tower cranes is in excess of 6 months and sometimes years, meaning construction companies must be both patient and clear about when they need a crane. Solutions to the problem are not forthcoming due to the difficulty in getting parts. China is the leading builder of crane parts, but will often need them to stay in China to support their own growth. 'House of Equipment', a construction equipment company in UAE currently receives requests daily for 6-12 cranes, which they simply cannot deliver. They already have 160 cranes standing.

PINK FLOYD ONCE CAUSED ALL FLIGHTS FROM HEATHROW TO BE CANCELLED

During the creation of Floyd's 'Animals' 1977 album cover, an accident involving a giant inflatable pig caused all flights to be grounded. The bassist was responsible for the idea of having a flying pig floating above an old Victorian-era power station near the airport. The giant pig was held to the roof with ropes. Before it could be photographed, the ropes snapped and the inflatable pig blew over into the airfield. Anecdotally, it was spotted by a 747 pilot flying at 40,000 feet. At 10pm the same night, a farmer rang the local police and asked if the pig could be collected, as it had landed in his field and was scaring the cows.

Fact 188

BEN & JERRY'S HAS A 'GRAVEYARD' FOR DISCONTINUED FLAVOURS

- - - - - - - - - - - - - - - - - - - -

Yes, Ben & Jerry's actually have a graveyard at their factory in Vermont, US. Each 'dead' flavour has its own tombstone containing information about the flavour and its years of life. If you can't make it to Vermont, the graveyard also features on the company's website. Once loved flavours include: This is nuts, Turtle soup, Vermonty Python, Crème Brûlée, Rainforest crunch, White Russian, Cool Britannia, and many more. You may not be so shocked to hear that Ben & Jerry's very first flavour was vanilla, which is still going strong today despite many rumours that it will be discontinued. The most popular flavour worldwide is chocolate chip cookie dough.

THE BOX JELLYFISH IS THE MOST POISONOUS ANIMAL IN THE WORLD

It is estimated that 50-100 people each year die as a result of being stung by a box jellyfish. The animal's body is covered with spines called 'nematocysts' filled with a toxic array of proteins, which when inflicted can cause death in a matter of minutes. Despite the number of deaths each year, not much is yet known about why the jellyfish's venom is so deadly, and there is also no antidote. People who are stung, often suffer from severe pain, local tissue death, and rapid heart rate followed by cardiovascular collapse. Interestingly, there are over 50 species of box jellyfish all producing a slightly different mix of toxins.

Fact 190

THE OLDEST LIVING LAND ANIMAL IS 190 YEARS OLD

■ ■ ■ ■ ■ ■ ■ ■ ■ ■ ■ ■ ■ ■ ■ ■ ■ ■ ■ ।

Johnathan the tortoise, is famed for being the oldest living land animal (verified). Johnathan is a resident of the British Atlantic island, St Helena, and has lived there in the grounds of his residence since being brought over in 1870. His species is native to the Seychelles and he is said to have lived there from birth in 1832, to 1870. Johnathan is now very old (even for a tortoise) and is both blind and can't smell. Despite the ailments, Johnathan is reportedly bisexual and still enjoys sex with the other male and female tortoises in the grounds of his residence. Johnathan's vet suggests that his sexual activity keeps him in good health. There is a lesson here for all of us.

27,000 TREES ARE CUT DOWN EACH DAY TO MAKE TOILET PAPER

The standard American goes through approximately 141 rolls of toilet paper per year. That's 28 lbs (12 kg) of paper. It is thought that each tree that is cut down can make up to 800 rolls of toilet paper. That's 14 trees worth of toilet paper used over a single lifetime. Luckily we now have many toilet paper brands which claim to be carbon neutral, and even carbon negative. Products are made from 100% bamboo or 100% recycled paper. Most of these companies also use no plastic. Packages are either biodegradable or can be recycled. The only problem with these brands is that they can be a little more pricey than your budget supermarket ranges.

Fact 192

APPLE SEEDS AND APRICOT PITS CONTAIN CYANIDE

■ ■ ■ ■ ■ ■ ■ ■ ■ ■ ■ ■ ■ ■ ■ ■ ▪

And in substantial amounts. Luckily, the cyanide is locked in a compound called amygdalin, and health cells lack enough of the enzyme required to convert it to cyanide, meaning the risk to human health is minimal. Still, it is recommended not to eat more than a couple of apricot pits per day just in case, as they contain the most amygdalin of all seeds. In contrast, some medical professionals have claimed that the release of cyanide from amygdalin can help prevent tumour formation, although more research is needed to verify this claim. It has certainly never cured anyone who has had cancer so far, and evaluating its effectiveness at preventing it would also be troublesome.

70% OF PEOPLE TILT THEIR HEAD TO THE RIGHT WHEN KISSING

Over two thirds of people will tilt their head to the right when going in for a kiss. But why does this happen? Studies have been conducted to find out whether this is innate or a learnt behaviour. Turns out that even toddlers have an innate urge to turn their head to the right in response to various (non-intimate) stimuli. It was also found that humans naturally like to see life 'play out' in a clockwise fashion. Without getting too scientific, this is said to be caused by the way the two hemispheres of the brain interact. Interestingly, this fact is true of all cultures, which strongly suggests it is not merely a learned behaviour. The kissing direction you choose is also linked to your writing hand preference.

Fact 194

26TH SEPTEMBER IS THE MOST COMMON BIRTHDAY

It is apparent that Christmas and new year are a good time to conceive, leading to a swathe of births in September and October. More babies are conceived in the UK and US in the weeks leading up to Christmas than any other time of year, making between the 17th and 30th of September the birth 'hotspot'. In contrast, the least common birthday is 25th December (provided you don't count 29th February that only happens once every four years). Another low birth day is 1st April, possibly due to parents not wanting to have an April fools baby. Interestingly, over the last two decades the average number of babies born in the US and UK is one every 48 seconds.

SCIENTISTS HAVE NO IDEA HOW DINOSAURS MATED

As animal fossils never come with soft tissues intact, it is near impossible to fathom what their sexual anatomy may have been like. Although, with new technology, and observations of birds and reptiles, we may be edging closer to an answer. Like crocodilians and birds of today, it is proposed that dinosaurs had a cloaca (a shared endpoint of the renal, digestive and reproductive systems). Such animals mate by connecting cloacae and passing sperm from male to female. This is known as a 'cloacal kiss'. Although this is generally accepted, the problem of sheer size and having a wide tail still casts some doubt on the exact logistics behind dinosaur lovemaking.

SELFIES ARE RESPONSIBLE FOR 43 DEATHS PER YEAR

The selfie craze which started back in 2010 has since yielded some interesting statistics regarding its safety. According to a scientific journal article and other sites, 259 selfie deaths occurred between 2011 and 2017. This figure comes from only 137 single incidents, meaning that more than one person died following each incident. The leading causes of selfie deaths are drowning (27%), falling (19.7%) and transportation (18.5%). The highest proportion of these accidents happened in India (60%) at tourist destinations. Some rare cases even involved fire, guns and electrocution. Finally, more males are likely to die taking selfies than females due to taking part in more risky behaviours.

Fact 197

WELL OVER 1,000 PEOPLE FLEE NORTH KOREA EVERY YEAR

■■■■■■■■■■■■■■■■■■■■

This is a modest number, as it only accounts for people arriving in the Democratic Republic of Korea. There will be many more who defect to China. In reality the numbers will be in thousands, maybe even tens of thousands. According to the 'Korean Ministry of Unification', 3,000 people fled to the South in 2009, making it the worst year in history. Interestingly, there was a sharp fall in escape attempts in 2012, the year when Kim Jong Un took office. The reason for this was mass media campaigns by Kim to display how difficult life was in the South for defectors, as well as having harsher border controls. Anyone caught will be subject to five years hard labour, torture, or imprisonment.

THERE ARE 5 PLACES IN THE WORLD CALLED 'HELL'

If you'd prefer not to wait until your time is up, you could always check out 'hell on Earth' to see what you think (and no, it isn't North Korea). Visiting every Hell in the world might even be a pleasant experience. From top to bottom, there is a hell in Nord-Trondelag in Norway, Gelderland in the Netherlands, Michigan in the US, and one in the Cayman Islands. There is also a 'Hel' in Northern Poland, but it's missing the final 'L' so we can't really count it. Although, it does have a novelty '666' numbered bus to take people to Hel and back. Other than the Cayman Islands, most of the Hells here on Earth rarely make it over 77°F (25°C) making them all the more hellish if you were to live there.

THE WORLD'S LONGEST CRUISE VISITS 150 DESTINATIONS IN 65 COUNTRIES

Royal Caribbean's 'Ultimate World Cruise' is due to set sail from Miami in December of 2023. The cruise will run for 274 days, stopping in 150 destinations in 65 countries across all seven continents. The cruise has a starting price (at the time of writing) of $59,999 per person for an inward facing room, plus $4,000 in taxes. Depending on your budget, you might want to upgrade to the Junior Suite from $117,599 per person plus taxes. There is a 10% discount offered for those who wish to pay upfront. Luckily if you can't afford to attend the entire cruise, you could join for a specific segment which comes in around the $15,000 mark. Do you need any more information?

KARATE ORIGINATED IN INDIA NOT CHINA OR JAPAN

■■■■■■■■■■■■■■■■■■■■■

The practice of karate follows a similar evolutionary path as Buddhism itself, through the teachings of Daruma (bodhidharma), its founder. Whilst living in Western India, Daruma devised a disciplinary regime in order to improve both mental and physical endurance in his disciples. He also wrote the first ever book on martial arts in 500 AD, named 'Ekkin-kyo'. As the story goes, Daruma visited the Shaolin temple in Northern China and passed on his teachings. From there, the practice spread to the islands of Okinawa, where they combined Daruma's teachings with their own form of open hand combat. This combination is said to form the basis of modern day Kung Fu and Karate.

MOST PEOPLE FART AROUND 15 TIMES PER DAY

Despite popular belief, this is the same for both men and women. This is of course an average, as the number of farts completely depends on diet and gut health. Although, if you fart 15 times per day, that's 5,476 farts per year, and 438,000 farts in the average lifetime (80 years). Each fart releases between 0.6 and 1.8 litres of gas. If you multiply this by the number of farts in a lifetime, you will likely pass a minimum of 262,000 litres (57,631 gallons) of gas and a maximum of 788,400 litres (173,423 gallons). Needless to say, there's a lot of wind being produced by the 8.05 billion people living on Earth, not to mention the cattle that feed us.

That's all for now. I hope you enjoyed reading

Interesting Facts for Curious Folk

AKNOWLEGEMENTS

Special thanks to the following websites for supplying factual inspiration and information.

www.rd.com
www.cosmopolitan.com
www.parade.com
www.thefactsite.com
www.wikipedia.com
www.britannica.com
www.pubmed.ncbi.nlm.nih.gov
www.which.co.uk
www.whatcar.com
www.guinnessworldrecords.com
www.who.com
www.nasa.gov
www.nhm.com
www.nationalgeographic.co.uk
www.ons.gov.uk
www.usa.gov

Printed in Great Britain
by Amazon

22393687R00116